READY FOR THE INTERVIEW

Lynne Weintraub

New Readers Press

Sample sections of the Application for Naturalization used in this text are taken from
Form N-400 (Rev. 03/26/16 N), available from the United States Citizenship and Immigration Services.

Citizenship: Passing the Test
Ready for the Interview
ISBN 978-1-56420-670-1

Copyright © 2016 New Readers Press
New Readers Press
ProLiteracy's Publishing Division
104 Marcellus Street., Syracuse, New York 13204
www.newreaderspress.com

Printed in the United States of America
10 9 8 7 6 5 4 3 2 1

Proceeds from the sale of New Readers Press materials support professional
development, training, and technical assistance programs of ProLiteracy
that benefit local literacy programs in the U.S. and around the globe.

Developmental Editor: Paula L. Schlusberg
Director of Design and Production: James P. Wallace
Cover Design: Carolyn Wallace
Illustrator: James P. Wallace
Photographer: Robert Mescavage
Technology Specialist: Maryellen Casey

Contents

Introduction

How to Use *Citizenship: Passing the Test: Ready for the Interview*

 Listen to This Information*

When you apply for U.S. citizenship, you complete an application form. Later, you have an interview with an examiner with the USCIS, the U.S. Citizenship and Immigration Services. To do these things, you need to understand spoken English.

This book and the *Citizenship* audio recording can help you. Practice listening to the English words as you read along in the book. You will get more comfortable and confident as you practice.

The citizenship application is Form N-400, Application for Naturalization. You fill it out and send it to the USCIS.

Citizenship: Passing the Test: Ready for the Interview can help you get ready to fill out the N-400 form. It shows how different people fill out their forms. And it lets you practice writing your own information on a blank form.

Later in the citizenship process, you will have an interview with a USCIS examiner. The examiner will
- ask questions about your application
- check if your answers match the answers on your application
- make sure you understand and speak English

Citizenship: Passing the Test: Ready for the Interview can also help you prepare for the interview. You can
- hear and read sample interviews
- hear and read different ways examiners ask for the same information
- hear and read how different people answer interview questions
- think about how you will answer interview questions
- practice listening to questions and answering them in English

After lots of practice, we hope you will feel confident and ready for your interview. Good luck!

But remember—the citizenship process can change over time. Be sure you have the most recent N-400 form. And be sure you know the current requirements for citizenship. If you have questions, get advice from an immigration specialist.

---

* When you see this symbol , play the *Citizenship* audio recording as you read along in the book.

Applying for Citizenship

What to Expect at the Interview

 ### Listen to the USCIS Examiner

Hello. My name is Mr. Cooper. I work at the U.S. Citizenship and Immigration Services (or USCIS). I'm a citizenship examiner.

Every day I interview many people. I ask the questions on the N-400 application. I check to see if there are any problems. I check to see if we need to make any changes in the application. I check to see if people are telling the truth.

Sometimes I look serious. I am trying to do my job quickly and carefully. Don't be afraid to talk to me.

If you don't understand a question, ask me to help you. Maybe I can repeat the question for you. Maybe I can ask the question in another way.

You need to speak and understand a little English. But it's OK if your English has some mistakes. You need to answer the questions, but you do not need to speak perfect English.

Are you getting ready for your interview? Read the questions on your N-400 application. Practice answering questions in English. If you practice, you will feel ready when you see me at the USCIS office.

Eligibility for Citizenship

 Listen to the USCIS Examiner

To become a citizen, you must be at least 18 years old. You must be a permanent resident. You must have a Permanent Resident Card or a green card. If your husband or wife is already a citizen, you can become a citizen after three years. If you are not married to a citizen, you can become a citizen after five years.

You must pass a test of U.S. history and government.* Most people must also speak, read, and write a little English.

Be careful! If you have left the United States for more than six months, you may need to wait before you send your application. If you lied to USCIS to get your green card, there could be a problem. If you have ever been arrested or put in jail, there could be a problem.

And here is the most important thing: You must promise to make the United States your number one country. You must promise to help your new country if there is an emergency.

---

* Some disabled people do not have to do this.

Benefits of Citizenship

Listen to Hai

 I want to be a citizen for many reasons. If I become a citizen, I can vote in elections. I can bring my family here from Vietnam. I can get an American passport. I can get a job with the U.S. government.

Someday maybe I will need help from the government.* If I become a citizen, I can apply for this help.

What Will Hai Say?

Why do you want to be a citizen?

_____ a. Because I want to get welfare and food stamps.

_____ b. Because I want to get a green card and a job.

_____ c. Because this is my country. I want to stay in America.

Hai's Interview

EXAMINER: Why do you want to be a citizen?

HAI: Because this is my country now. I want to stay in America. And I want to vote.

What Will You Say?

Why do you want to be a citizen?

---

* Some examples are food stamps, welfare, or SSI (disability).

Filling Out the N-400 Application

 ## Listen to the USCIS Examiner

 There are two ways you can fill out your N-400 form. You can type it by computer and then print out the form. The computer will make sure you enter the information in the correct format.

Or you can get a blank form and fill it out with a black pen. Be sure to print clearly.

Start the form by entering your A-Number. This is the number on your Permanent Resident Card—your green card. The number begins with the letter A. There should be nine numbers after the A. If the A-Number has eight numbers, put a 0 before the first number.

You may still have an old green card. Or you may have a new card. The cards have different formats. But they both have your A-Number.

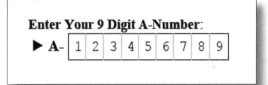

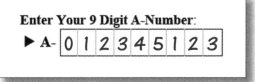

If you need more space to write any of your answers, use a separate piece of paper. At the top of the paper, write your name, your A-Number, and "N-400." Then write the number of the question you are answering.

Listen to Hai

 I am applying to be a citizen. My sister Lin wants to be a citizen too. We want to go to our interviews on the same day.

I wrote a note to USCIS:

Dear USCIS,
We would like to be interviewed on the same day, if it is possible.
Hai Pham A#234567890
Lin Pham A#234567891

Thank you.
Hai Pham
Lin Pham

We put our applications together in one envelope.

Maybe our appointments will be on different days. But maybe USCIS will give us appointments on the same day. We hope that USCIS will be able to take us together.

The Application Fee

Listen to Susan

It costs a lot of money to apply for citizenship. I have saved some money out of each paycheck for 12 months. Now I have enough money to pay the application fee. I checked the website at www.USCIS.gov to find out how much money to send. You can send a personal check or a money order with your application. I decided to write a personal check. I made it out to the *U.S. Department of Homeland Security*. I signed the check. In the corner, I wrote *N-400 application fee.*

SUSAN SANTOS   301
37 Lincoln Street
Bridgeport, CT 01048

December 13   20 16

Pay to   U.S. Department of Homeland Security $ 680.00

Six hundred eighty and 00/100 ～～～～～ DOLLARS

First City Bank
Bridgeport, CT 01048

Memo N-400 Application Fee   *Susan Santos*

Listen to Chong

I am a single mother, and my job doesn't pay much. I don't have enough money to pay the application fee. I looked on the USCIS.gov website and I learned that if you are poor, you can ask for a fee waiver. If you qualify for food stamps or other "means tested" benefits, you can ask for a waiver. Or you can look at form I-912P and see if your family income is below the poverty guidelines. I filled out the fee waiver request form I-912. I got a copy of a recent food stamps determination letter. I sent them with my N-400 application.

A few weeks later I got a notice that USCIS received my application. In the notice, it said that the fee I paid was $0. That is how I knew that USCIS accepted my fee waiver request.

The Application Process

🔘 Listen to Maria

This year, I decided to apply for citizenship. I filled out an N-400 application. I wrote my A-Number at the top of each page. Then I signed the form.

I got photographs and a check to send with my application. I also sent a copy of the front and back of my green card. I made a copy of the application to keep for myself.

Soon, I got a letter back. It said my application arrived OK at USCIS.

A few weeks later, I got another letter. It told me where and when to get my fingerprints taken.

Then I waited for an interview appointment. After a few more weeks, USCIS sent me an interview notice. The notice told me where and when to go for my interview.

U.S. Department of Homeland Security
Citizenship and Immigration Services

I-797C, Notice of Action

THE UNITED STATES OF AMERICA

Request for Applicant to Appear for Naturalization Initial Interview			NOTICE DATE 11/18/2016
CASE TYPE N400 Application for Naturalization			FILE or A# A 12 345 123
APPLICATION NUMBER NBC	RECEIVED DATE 6/30/2016	PRIORITY DATE 6/30/2016	PAGE 1 of 1

APPLICANT NAME AND MAILING ADDRESS

MARIA ELENA PEREZ
419 MAIN ST APT 122
DALLAS, TX 75208

ılıllıllııılıl

Please come to:
CITIZENSHIP AND IMMIGRATION SERVICES
8101 N. STEMMONS FREEWAY
DALLAS, TX 75247

Date   12/12/2016
Time   10:00 AM

You are hereby notified to appear for an interview on your application for naturalization at the DATE, TIME and PLACE, shown above. **Waiting room capacity is limited. Please do not arrive any earlier than 30 minutes before your scheduled appointment time.** The proceeding will take about 2 hours. If for any reason you cannot keep this appointment, please return it immediately to the Citizenship office listed above with your explanation and a request for a new appointment: otherwise no further action will be taken.

I practiced for my interview. I looked at my N-400 application to remember the information. I listened to interview questions and practiced answering in English.

Today I will go to my interview. I decided to wear a nice dress. I remembered to bring my interview notice. I also have my passport, my green card, and my driver's license.

Now I am ready for my interview.

Getting Started at the Interview

Responding to Commands and Taking an Oath

Maria's Interview

Listen to the USCIS Examiner

 What will you do at your interview? Find a picture to go with the words.

1. Put your interview notice on the stack.
2. Please wait. Someone will call you.
3. Follow me.
4. Please come in.
5. Remain standing.
6. Raise your right hand.

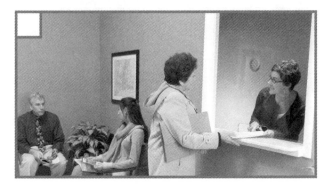

7. You may sit down.

8. Show me your green card.

9. I have an interview for citizenship today.

10. Sign your name.

N-400 Part 1
Information About Your Eligibility

Listen to Maria

 To become a citizen, you have to be a lawful permanent resident for five years or longer. I have been a permanent resident since 2005. I came to the U.S. in 2005. I got my green card more than five years ago.

Maria's Form

Part 1. Information About Your Eligibility (Select only one box or your Form N-400 may be delayed)	Enter Your 9 Digit A-Number: ▶ A- 0 1 2 3 4 5 1 2 3

1. You are at least 18 years of age **and:**

   A. ✓ Have been a lawful permanent resident of the United States for at least 5 years.

   B. ☐ Have been a lawful permanent resident of the United States for at least 3 years. In addition, you have been married to and living with the same U.S. citizen spouse for the last 3 years, **and** your spouse has been a U.S. citizen for the last 3 years at the time you filed your Form N-400.

   C. ☐ Are a lawful permanent resident of the United States **and** you are the spouse of a U.S. citizen **and** your U.S. citizen spouse is regularly engaged in specified employment abroad. (See the Immigration and Nationality Act (INA) section 319(b).) If your residential address is outside the United States and you are filing under Section 319(b), select the USCIS Field Office from the list below where you would like to have your naturalization interview:

   [   ]

   D. ☐ Are applying on the basis of qualifying military service.

   E. ☐ Other (Explain): [   ]

What Will Maria Say?

How long have you been a permanent resident?

_____ a. Since 2005.

_____ b. I have a green card.

_____ c. Yes, I am.

Maria's Interview

EXAMINER: Let's see. You've been a permanent resident since 2005. Is that right?

MARIA: Permanent resident? Can you say it again?

EXAMINER: How long have you been a permanent resident?

MARIA: Oh. Since 2005.

◉ Listen to Susan

Three years ago, I married a U.S. citizen. I am still married. I have been married to a citizen for three years.

Three years ago, I got my green card. I have been a permanent resident for three years. I have lived in the U.S. with my husband for the whole three years.

I can apply for citizenship after only three years.

Susan's Form

Part 1. Information About Your Eligibility (Select only one box or your Form N-400 may be delayed)	Enter Your 9 Digit A-Number: ▶ A- 0 8 9 0 1 2 6 5 4

1. You are at least 18 years of age **and:**

   A. ☐ Have been a lawful permanent resident of the United States for at least 5 years.

   B. ☒ Have been a lawful permanent resident of the United States for at least 3 years. In addition, you have been married to and living with the same U.S. citizen spouse for the last 3 years, **and** your spouse has been a U.S. citizen for the last 3 years at the time you filed your Form N-400.

   C. ☐ Are a lawful permanent resident of the United States **and** you are the spouse of a U.S. citizen **and** your U.S. citizen spouse is regularly engaged in specified employment abroad. (See the Immigration and Nationality Act (INA) section 319(b).) If your residential address is outside the United States and you are filing under Section 319(b), select the USCIS Field Office from the list below where you would like to have your naturalization interview:

   [   ]

   D. ☐ Are applying on the basis of qualifying military service.

   E. ☐ Other (Explain): [   ]

What Will Susan Say?

You've been a permanent resident for three years, is that right?

_____ a. Yes.

_____ b. Permanent resident.

_____ c. 2013.

Susan's Interview

EXAMINER:	You've been a permanent resident for three years, is that right?
SUSAN:	Yes.
EXAMINER:	So you're eligible for citizenship based on marriage to a citizen.
SUSAN:	Yes.
EXAMINER:	How long have you been married?
SUSAN:	Three years.
EXAMINER:	And you're still married? No change?
SUSAN:	Yes, I'm still married.
EXAMINER:	When did your spouse become a citizen?
SUSAN:	Spouse?
EXAMINER:	Your husband. When did he become a citizen?
SUSAN:	In 2008.
EXAMINER:	Do you currently live with your spouse?
SUSAN:	My husband? Yes.
EXAMINER:	And you've lived with him continuously since you were married?
SUSAN:	Continuously?
EXAMINER:	Did you live with him the whole time—for the full three years?
SUSAN:	Yes, that's right.

What Will You Say?

How long have you been a permanent resident?
How many years have you had your green card?
How many years have you had your permanent resident card?

When did you become a permanent resident?
When did you get your permanent resident card?

Questions About a U.S. Citizen Spouse

- Is your application based on marriage to a citizen?

- How long has your spouse been a citizen?

- When did your spouse become a citizen?

- Are you currently married?

- When did you get married?

- Are you still married?

- How long have you been married?

- Are you still living with your spouse?

- How long have you lived with your spouse?

- Have you lived with your spouse continuously for the last three years?

Your Form

Part 1. Information About Your Eligibility (Select only one box or your Form N-400 may be delayed)

Enter Your 9 Digit A-Number:
► A-

1. You are at least 18 years of age **and:**

   A. ☐ Have been a lawful permanent resident of the United States for at least 5 years.

   B. ☐ Have been a lawful permanent resident of the United States for at least 3 years. In addition, you have been married to and living with the same U.S. citizen spouse for the last 3 years, **and** your spouse has been a U.S. citizen for the last 3 years at the time you filed your Form N-400.

   C. ☐ Are a lawful permanent resident of the United States **and** you are the spouse of a U.S. citizen **and** your U.S. citizen spouse is regularly engaged in specified employment abroad. (See the Immigration and Nationality Act (INA) section 319(b).) If your residential address is outside the United States and you are filing under Section 319(b), select the USCIS Field Office from the list below where you would like to have your naturalization interview:

   D. ☐ Are applying on the basis of qualifying military service.

   E. ☐ Other (Explain):

N-400 Part 2
Information About You

Your Current Legal Name

 Listen to Maria

 My name is Maria Elena Perez. My last name is Perez. I'm Mrs. Perez. My husband was Mr. Perez. Perez is our family name.

My first name is Maria. Everyone calls me Maria. Maria is my given name.

My middle name is Elena.

Maria's Form

Part 2. Information About You (Person applying for naturalization)
1. Your Current Legal Name (**do not** provide a nickname)

Family Name (Last Name)	Given Name (First Name)	Middle Name (if applicable)
Perez	Maria	Elena

What Will Maria Say?

So your family name is Perez. How do you spell it?

_____ a. Perez.

_____ b. P-E-R-E-Z.

_____ c. Maria Elena Perez.

Maria's Interview

EXAMINER: So your family name is Perez. How do you spell it?

MARIA: P-E-R-E-Z.

EXAMINER: OK. Your given name is Maria?

MARIA: Yes.

EXAMINER: And your middle name is, let's see . . . Elena—is that right?

MARIA: Yes.

Listen to Hai

 My full name is Hai Pham. My family name is Pham. All of my brothers and sisters have the same family name. We are the Pham family.

My given name is Hai. I don't have a middle name.

Hai's Form

Part 2. **Information About You** (Person applying for naturalization)

1. Your Current Legal Name (**do not** provide a nickname)

Family Name (Last Name)	Given Name (First Name)	Middle Name (if applicable)
PHAM	HAI	N/A

What Will Hai Say?

Could you state your full name, please?

_____ a. P-H-A-M.

_____ b. Full name.

_____ c. Hai Pham.

Hai's Interview

EXAMINER: Could you state your full name, please?

HAI: Hai Pham.

EXAMINER: Pham is the family name?

HAI: Yes.

EXAMINER: How do you spell it?

HAI: P-H-A-M.

EXAMINER: No middle name?

HAI: No.

◉ What Will You Say?

State your full name, please.
What is your full name?

What's your family name?
What's your last name?

What's your first name?
What's your given name?

How do you spell that?
Could you spell your last name for me?

Do you have a middle name?
What's your middle name?

Your Form

Part 2. Information About You (Person applying for naturalization)		
1. Your Current Legal Name (**do not** provide a nickname)		
Family Name (Last Name)	Given Name (First Name)	Middle Name (if applicable)

The Name on Your Permanent Resident Card

Listen to Maria

 My current legal name is Maria Elena Perez. Perez was my husband's name. That's the name I use now. That name goes in section 1.

But my green card has a different name. In Mexico, I kept Cruz as my last name when I married. Cruz was my father's name. It's my maiden name. That's the name I used on my green card. In section 2, I copied the name exactly as it is on my green card.

Maria's Form

Part 2. Information About You (Person applying for naturalization)		
1. Your Current Legal Name (**do not** provide a nickname)		
Family Name (Last Name)	Given Name (First Name)	Middle Name (if applicable)
Perez	Maria	Elena
2. Your Name Exactly As It Appears on Your Permanent Resident Card (if applicable)		
Family Name (Last Name)	Given Name (First Name)	Middle Name (if applicable)
Cruz	Maria	Elena

What Will Maria Say?

Your green card says "Maria Elena Cruz," right?

_____ a. No. My name is Maria.

_____ b. Yes.

_____ c. My last name is Perez.

Maria's Interview

EXAMINER: You are currently using a different name than the one on your Permanent Resident Card. Is that correct?

MARIA: I'm sorry. Can you say that more slowly?

EXAMINER: OK, your Permanent Resident Card—your green card—says Maria Elena Cruz, right?

MARIA: Yes.

EXAMINER: But you now use the name Maria Elena Perez.

MARIA: Yes, Perez. In the U.S. I use my married name, Perez.

Other Names

 Listen to Hai

 My name is Hai Pham. That is the name my mother and father gave to me. I have used that name since I was born. I have never used any other name.

Hai's Form

Part 2. Information About You (Person applying for naturalization)

1. Your Current Legal Name (**do not** provide a nickname)

Family Name (Last Name)	Given Name (First Name)	Middle Name (if applicable)
PHAM	HAI	N/A

2. Your Name Exactly As It Appears on Your Permanent Resident Card (if applicable)

Family Name (Last Name)	Given Name (First Name)	Middle Name (if applicable)
PHAM	HAI	N/A

Part 2. Information About You (Person applying for naturalization) (continued)

3. Other Names You Have Used Since Birth (include nicknames, aliases, and maiden name, if applicable)

Family Name (Last Name)	Given Name (First Name)	Middle Name (if applicable)
N/A	N/A	N/A

What Will Hai Say?

Have you used any other names since you came here?

_____ a. No, just one name.

_____ b. Hai Pham.

_____ c. Yes, my name is Hai.

Hai's Interview

EXAMINER:	Now, the name you've used here is Hai Pham. Have you used any other names since you came here?
HAI:	No.
EXAMINER:	You don't go by any other names?
HAI:	Could you please repeat the question?
EXAMINER:	Have you ever used another name?
HAI:	No, just one name, all my life.

Listen to Nick

When I was born, my mother named me On Pick. My mother died when I was 7 years old. I came to America when I was 11 years old. I came here alone.

I lived with an American family, the Hill family. Later they adopted me, and I changed my name. Now I use an American name. My American name is Nick Hill.

Nick Hill is my legal name now. It's the name on my ID cards, and it's the name I use when I sign papers.

When I sent my application to USCIS, I sent a copy of my adoption papers.

Nick's Form

Part 2. **Information About You** (Person applying for naturalization)		
1. Your Current Legal Name (**do not** provide a nickname)		
Family Name (Last Name)	Given Name (First Name)	Middle Name (if applicable)
Hill	Nick	N/A
2. Your Name Exactly As It Appears on Your Permanent Resident Card (if applicable)		
Family Name (Last Name)	Given Name (First Name)	Middle Name (if applicable)
Pick	On	N/A

What Will Nick Say?

You seem to be using a different name than the one on your green card. Why is that?

_____ a. I changed my name.

_____ b. My name is Nick Hill.

_____ c. My green card has the name On Pick.

Nick's Interview

EXAMINER: Now, you seem to be using a different name than the one on your permanent resident card. Why is that?

NICK: I changed my name when I was adopted.

EXAMINER: So Nick Hill is your current legal name?

NICK: Current?

EXAMINER: Is Nick Hill your legal name now?

NICK: Yes.

Listen to Lisa

 My Chinese name is Xia-Zheng Chen. My passport and my green card say Xia-Zheng Chen. That's my current legal name. But in the United States some people have trouble saying my name. So now I use the name Lisa Chen. Lisa is my nickname.

Lisa's Form

Part 2. Information About You (Person applying for naturalization)

1. Your Current Legal Name (**do not** provide a nickname)

Family Name (Last Name)	Given Name (First Name)	Middle Name (if applicable)
Chen	Xia-Zheng	N/A

2. Your Name Exactly As It Appears on Your Permanent Resident Card (if applicable)

Family Name (Last Name)	Given Name (First Name)	Middle Name (if applicable)
Chen	Xia-Zheng	N/A

Part 2. Information About You (Person applying for naturalization) (continued)

3. Other Names You Have Used Since Birth (include nicknames, aliases, and maiden name, if applicable)

Family Name (Last Name)	Given Name (First Name)	Middle Name (if applicable)
Chen	Lisa	N/A

What Will Lisa Say?

Have you ever gone to court to change your name?

_____ a. No.

_____ b. It's easier to say.

_____ c. L-I-S-A.

🔘 Lisa's Interview

EXAMINER: You have two names listed on your application form, Xia-Zheng Chen and Lisa Chen. What is the reason for that?

LISA: My Chinese name is Xia-Zheng. But I use the name Lisa in the U.S. because Lisa is easier for some people to say.

EXAMINER: Which one is your legal name?

LISA: Legal?

EXAMINER: Have you gone to court to change your name to Lisa Chen?

LISA: No.

EXAMINER: Then Xia-Zheng Chen is your legal name, for now.

🔘 What Will You Say?

Please state your full legal name.
What is your current legal name?

Have you used any other names since you came here?
Have you used any other names since you became a permanent resident?
Do you go by any other names?
What other names have you used?
Have you ever changed your name?

Your Form

Part 2. Information About You (Person applying for naturalization)		
1. Your Current Legal Name (**do not** provide a nickname)		
Family Name (Last Name)	Given Name (First Name)	Middle Name (if applicable)
2. Your Name Exactly As It Appears on Your Permanent Resident Card (if applicable)		
Family Name (Last Name)	Given Name (First Name)	Middle Name (if applicable)

Part 2. Information About You (Person applying for naturalization) (continued)		
3. Other Names You Have Used Since Birth (include nicknames, aliases, and maiden name, if applicable)		
Family Name (Last Name)	Given Name (First Name)	Middle Name (if applicable)

Name Change

Listen to Lisa

 When you become a citizen, you can take a new name. I want my citizenship papers to say Lisa Xia-Zheng Chen. I want to change my name.

Lisa's Form

4.   Name Change (Optional)

Read the Form N-400 Instructions before you decide whether or not you would like to legally change your name.

Would you like to legally change your name?   ☒ Yes ☐ No

If you answered "Yes," type or print the new name you would like to use in the spaces provided below.

Family Name (Last Name)	Given Name (First Name)	Middle Name (if applicable)
Chen	Lisa	Xia Zheng

What Will Lisa Say?

What name do you want to use after you become a citizen?

_____ a. Yes, I do.

_____ b. Next year.

_____ c. Lisa Xia-Zheng Chen.

Lisa's Interview

EXAMINER: Your application says you want to change your name. What name do you want to use after you become a citizen?

LISA: Lisa Xia-Zheng Chen.

Listen to Hai

 I don't want a new name. I want to keep my name the same.

Hai's Form

4. Name Change (Optional)

Read the Form N-400 Instructions before you decide whether or not you would like to legally change your name.

Would you like to legally change your name? ☐ Yes ☒ No

If you answered "Yes," type or print the new name you would like to use in the spaces provided below.

Family Name (Last Name)	Given Name (First Name)	Middle Name (if applicable)

What Will Hai Say?

Do you want to change your name?

_____ a. No, I don't.

_____ b. Hai Pham.

_____ c. Yes, the same.

Hai's Interview

EXAMINER: Some people change their names when they become U.S. citizens. Do you want to change your name?

HAI: No, I don't.

 **What Will You Say?**

Do you want to change your name?
Would you like to change your name?

What name do you want to use when you become a citizen?
What name do you want on your naturalization certificate?

Your Form

4. Name Change (Optional)

    Read the Form N-400 Instructions before you decide whether or not you would like to legally change your name.

    Would you like to legally change your name?   ☐ Yes ☐ No

    If you answered "Yes," type or print the new name you would like to use in the spaces provided below.

Family Name (Last Name)	Given Name (First Name)	Middle Name (if applicable)

Social Security Number, Gender, and Dates

Listen to Hai

 I wrote my Social Security number on my application. I don't have a USCIS online account. So I didn't write anything in number 6.

I am a man, so I checked the box that says, "Male." My sister is a woman, so she will check the box that says, "Female."

In the U.S., people write the month first, the day next, and the year last. My date of birth is November 7, 1979. I wrote the date like this: 11/07/1979.

The date I became a permanent resident was July 8, 2003. I wrote the date like this: 07/08/2003.

Hai's Form

5. U.S. Social Security Number (if applicable) ► 1 2 7 4 0 1 8 3 7	**6.** USCIS Online Account Number (if any) ►	
7. Gender ☒ Male ☐ Female	**8.** Date of Birth (mm/dd/yyyy) 11/07/1979	**9.** Date You Became a Lawful Permanent Resident (mm/dd/yyyy) 07/08/2003

What Will Hai Say?

Your date of birth is November 7, 1977, is that correct?

_____ a. No, it's 1979.

_____ b. No, my Social Security number.

_____ c. No, in Vietnam.

Hai's Interview

EXAMINER: What's your Social Security number?

HAI: 127-40-1837.

EXAMINER: And your date of birth is November 7, 1977, is that correct?

HAI: No, it's 1979.

EXAMINER: 1979 . . . OK.

Listen to Hai

If you look carefully on your green card, you can find the date you became a permanent resident. I came to the U.S. on July 8, 2003. I became a permanent resident on the day I arrived in the U.S.

Hai's Green Card

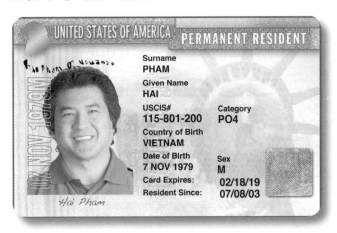

Hai's Form

9. Date You Became a Lawful Permanent Resident (mm/dd/yyyy)

07/08/2003

Listen to Maria

I came to the U.S. as an immigrant on September 27, 2005. I became a permanent resident on the day I arrived in the U.S.

Maria's Green Card

Maria's Form

9. Date You Became a Lawful Permanent Resident (mm/dd/yyyy)

09/27/2005

Listen to Chong

 I came to the U.S. as a tourist in 1999. I did not have a green card then. I was not a permanent resident. In 2003 I got an adjustment of status. That's when I became a permanent resident. That's when I got my green card.

Chong's Green Card

UNITED STATES OF AMERICA   PERMANENT RESIDENT

Surname
BARTON
Given Name
CHONG
USCIS#
098-765-432
Category
PO4
Country of Birth
KOREA
Date of Birth
14 FEB 1980
Sex
F
Card Expires: **05/09/20**
Resident Since: **06/07/03**

Chong Barton

Chong's Form

9.   Date You Became a Lawful
     Permanent Resident (mm/dd/yyyy)

     06/07/2003

What Will Chong Say?

When did you get your green card?

_____ a. In Los Angeles.

_____ b. Permanent resident.

_____ c. In 2003.

Chong's Interview

EXAMINER: When you arrived in the United States, you were not a permanent resident. Is that right?

CHONG: Yes. I came on a tourist visa.

EXAMINER: When did you get an adjustment of status?

CHONG: What did you say?

EXAMINER: When did you become a permanent resident? When did you get your green card?

CHONG: Uh . . . that was in 2003.

◉ What Will You Say?

Do you know your Social Security number?
What is your Social Security number?

What's your date of birth?
When were you born?

Can you tell me the date you became a permanent resident?
When did you become a permanent resident?
When did you get your green card?

Your Form

5.	U.S. Social Security Number (if applicable)	6.	USCIS Online Account Number (if any)
▶		▶	

7.	Gender	8.	Date of Birth (mm/dd/yyyy)	9.	Date You Became a Lawful Permanent Resident (mm/dd/yyyy)
	☐ Male ☐ Female				

Country of Birth/Country of Nationality

Listen to Maria

 I was born in Mexico. Mexico is my country of birth. I am a citizen of Mexico right now. My country of nationality is Mexico.

Maria's Form

10. Country of Birth	11. Country of Citizenship or Nationality
Mexico	Mexico

What Will Maria Say?

So you're a citizen of Mexico?

_____ a. My country.

_____ b. I want to be a U.S. citizen.

_____ c. That's right.

Maria's Interview

EXAMINER: What's your country of nationality?

MARIA: Mexico.

EXAMINER: So you are a citizen of Mexico?

MARIA: Yes, that's right.

Listen to Nick

 I was born in a refugee camp in Thailand. But I am not a citizen of Thailand.

My parents were from Cambodia. I am Cambodian. Cambodia is my country of nationality.

Nick's Form

10. Country of Birth	11. Country of Citizenship or Nationality
Thailand	Cambodia

What Will Nick Say?

Is Thailand your country of nationality?

_____ a. No, I'm a Cambodian citizen.

_____ b. Yes, I was born in Thailand.

_____ c. I want to be an American.

Nick's Interview

EXAMINER: Your application says you were born in Thailand.

NICK: Yes, that's right.

EXAMINER: Is Thailand your country of nationality?

NICK: No, I'm a Cambodian citizen.

What Will You Say?

What is your country of birth?
Where were you born?
In which country were you born?

What is your country of nationality?
Are you a citizen of any other country?

Your Form

10. Country of Birth	11. Country of Citizenship or Nationality

Disability Waivers

 ## Listen to Hai

 My sister Lin is disabled. It is very hard for her to learn new things. She forgets many things I tell her. Her doctor says that she will always need special help.

When I applied to become a citizen, Lin wanted to be a citizen too. So Lin's doctor filled out a form called N-648. The doctor explained the medical reasons for Lin's problem. She explained why Lin cannot study for a test. If the USCIS examiner agrees with the doctor, Lin will not have to take a test. I will help her when she has her interview. She will become a citizen too.

Lin's Form

12. Do you have a physical or developmental disability or mental impairment that prevents you from demonstrating your knowledge and understanding of the English language and/or civics requirements for naturalization?	☒ Yes ☐ No

If you answered "Yes," submit a completed Form N-648, Medical Certification for Disability Exceptions, when you file your Form N-400.

Test Exemptions

 ## Listen to the USCIS Examiner

 To become a citizen, most people have to show me that they know a little English. But there are a few exceptions for older people who have lived in the U.S. for a long time. They do not have to take an English test. They can have a translator at their interview. But they still have to answer questions about U.S. history and government.

You can qualify for this exception if you have lived in the U.S. as a permanent resident for more than 20 years, and you are more than 50 years old. You can also qualify if you have lived in the U.S. as a permanent resident for more than 15 years, and you are more than 55 years old.

There's one more exception for elderly people. If you have been a permanent resident for more than 20 years, and you're more than 65 years old, you can also take an easier test of U.S. history and government.

But there's one thing to keep in mind. You have to meet these qualifications before you can send in your N-400 application form.

Your Form

13. Exemptions from the English Language Test

    A. Are you **50** years of age or older **and** have you lived in the United States as a lawful permanent resident for periods totaling at least **20** years at the time you file your Form N-400? ☐ Yes ☐ No

    B. Are you **55** years of age or older **and** have you lived in the United States as a lawful permanent resident for periods totaling at least **15** years at the time you file your Form N-400? ☐ Yes ☐ No

    C. Are you **65** years of age or older **and** have you lived in the United States as a lawful permanent resident for periods totaling at least **20** years at the time you file your Form N-400? (If you meet this requirement, you will also be given a simplified version of the civics test.) ☐ Yes ☐ No

N-400 Part 3
Accommodations for Individuals With Disabilities

 Listen to Otto

 I am 72 years old. My ears are not strong anymore. Sometimes I cannot hear what people say to me. I have been getting ready for my interview for a long time. But I do not know if I will be able to hear the examiner's questions. I'm asking for a small change in the way the examiner does the interview.

If you have a disability, you can write about it in your application. You can suggest a way for the examiner to make the interview easier for you. You can ask for an accommodation.

I am asking the examiner to let my daughter go with me to my interview. If I cannot hear a question, my daughter will repeat the question close to my ear. Sometimes I can hear my daughter better than I can hear other people.

Otto's Form

Part 3. Accommodations for Individuals With Disabilities and/or Impairments

NOTE: Read the information in the Form N-400 Instructions before completing this part.

1. Are you requesting an accommodation because of your disabilities and/or impairments? ☒ Yes ☐ No

If you answered "Yes," select any applicable box.

A. ☒ I am deaf or hard of hearing and request the following accommodation. (If you are requesting a sign-language interpreter, indicate for which language (for example, American Sign Language).)

Allow my daughter to repeat questions in my ear if I have trouble hearing

B. ☐ I am blind or have low vision and request the following accommodation:

N-400 Part 4
Information to Contact You

Listen to Susan

 On the day that my interview was supposed to happen, there was a big snowstorm. I got a phone call from USCIS. A woman told me that my appointment was cancelled. She said that I would get a new appointment notice in a few weeks.

It's a good thing that I wrote my cell phone number on my N-400 application. I'm glad I did not try to drive to the USCIS office on icy roads!

Susan's Form

Part 4. Information to Contact You

1. Daytime Telephone Number	2. Work Telephone Number (if any)	
2322322211	2341192323	
3. Evening Telephone Number	4. Mobile Telephone Number (if any)	
	3452349090	
5. Email Address (if any)		
ssantos34@rgn.com		

Your Form

Part 4. Information to Contact You

1. Daytime Telephone Number	2. Work Telephone Number (if any)
3. Evening Telephone Number	4. Mobile Telephone Number (if any)
5. Email Address (if any)	

Information About Your Residence

Home Address

 Listen to Maria

 I live in an apartment building. It's at 419 Main Street. My home address is 419 Main Street. That's my current physical address. My apartment number is 122.

Maria's Form

Part 5. Information About Your Residence

1. Where have you lived during the last five years? Provide your most recent residence and then list every location where you have lived during the last five years. If you need extra space, use additional sheets of paper.

   A. Current Physical Address

   Street Number and Name

   | 419 Main St. | Apt. ☑ | Ste. ☐ | Flr. ☐ | Number 122 |

What Will Maria Say?

What's your current address?

_____ a. Texas.

_____ b. 419 Main Street, Apartment 122.

_____ c. I live in an apartment.

 Maria's Interview

EXAMINER: What's your current address?

MARIA: Uh . . . current?

EXAMINER: What is your address right now?

MARIA: 419 Main Street, Apartment 122.

Listen to Susan

I live in Bridgeport, Connecticut. My city is Bridgeport. But I didn't know what county Bridgeport is in.

If you don't know, you have to ask somebody. I asked my neighbor, but she didn't know either. Then I asked the mailman. He told me Bridgeport is in Fairfield County. He told me how to spell it: F-A-I-R-F-I-E-L-D.

Bridgeport is in Connecticut. Connecticut is my state. I know my zip code. It's 01048. I have lived in Bridgeport since June 15, 2014.

Susan's Form

Part 5. Information About Your Residence

1. Where have you lived during the last five years? Provide your most recent residence and then list every location where you have lived during the last five years. If you need extra space, use additional sheets of paper.

   A. Current Physical Address

   Street Number and Name | Apt. Ste. Flr. Number

   `37 Lincoln St` ☐ ☐ ☐

City or Town	County	State	ZIP Code + 4
`Bridgeport`	`Fairfield`	`CT`	`01048` - `1234`

Province or Region (foreign address only)	Postal Code (foreign address only)	Country (foreign address only)
		`USA`

   Dates of Residence | From (mm/dd/yyyy) `06/15/2014` | To (mm/dd/yyyy) `Present`

What Will Susan Say?

Do you still live in Bridgeport, Connecticut?

_____ a. Yes, Bridgeport.

_____ b. Fairfield County.

_____ c. My city and state.

Susan's Interview

EXAMINER: Do you still live in Bridgeport, Connecticut?

SUSAN: Yes, Bridgeport.

EXAMINER: So that's . . . Fairfield County?

SUSAN: Yes, Fairfield County.

Listen to Lisa

I have two addresses. I live at 154 Glendale Avenue. That's my street address. But I get my mail at the post office. My mailing address is P.O. Box 1658.

Lisa's Form

Part 5. Information About Your Residence

1. Where have you lived during the last five years? Provide your most recent residence and then list every location where you have lived during the last five years. If you need extra space, use additional sheets of paper.

A. Current Physical Address

Street Number and Name | Apt. ☐ Ste. ☐ Flr. ☐ Number ☐

154 Glendale Ave

City or Town	County	State	ZIP Code + 4
Riverdale	Morris	NJ	07457 - 1432

Province or Region (foreign address only) | Postal Code (foreign address only) | Country (foreign address only)

| | | USA |

Dates of Residence | From (mm/dd/yyyy) 11/01/2008 | To (mm/dd/yyyy) Present

B. Current Mailing Address (if different from the address above)

In Care Of Name (if any)

Street Number and Name | Apt. ☐ Ste. ☐ Flr. ☐ Number ☐

PO Box 1658

City or Town	County	State	ZIP Code + 4
Riverdale	Morris	NJ	07457 - 1658

Province or Region (foreign address only) | Postal Code (foreign address only) | Country (foreign address only)

| | | USA |

What Will Lisa Say?

What is your street address?

_____ a. P.O. Box 1658.

_____ b. Riverdale, New Jersey.

_____ c. 154 Glendale Avenue.

 ## Lisa's Interview

EXAMINER: Are you still receiving mail at P.O. Box 1658?

LISA: Yes.

EXAMINER: And what is your street address?

LISA: 154 Glendale Avenue, Riverdale, New Jersey.

EXAMINER: Is that in Passaic County?

LISA: No. It's Morris County.

What Will You Say?

Where do you live?
What is your current address?
What is your street address?
What is your current physical address?

What is your city?
What city do you live in?

What is your state?
What state are you in?

What's your zip code?

Which county is that?

Has your address changed since you sent in your application?

Do you have a different mailing address?
What's your mailing address?
Where do you receive mail?

Your Form

Part 5. Information About Your Residence

1. Where have you lived during the last five years? Provide your most recent residence and then list every location where you have lived during the last five years. If you need extra space, use additional sheets of paper.

A. Current Physical Address

Street Number and Name   Apt. Ste. Flr. Number

City or Town   County   State   ZIP Code + 4

Province or Region (foreign address only)   Postal Code (foreign address only)   Country (foreign address only)

Dates of Residence   From (mm/dd/yyyy)   To (mm/dd/yyyy)

B. Current Mailing Address (if different from the address above)

In Care Of Name (if any)

Street Number and Name   Apt. Ste. Flr. Number

City or Town   County   State   ZIP Code + 4

Province or Region (foreign address only)   Postal Code (foreign address only)   Country (foreign address only)

Former Address

Listen to Hai

 I have lived at the same address since October 2006. In the last five years, I had only one address. If your address changes after you send your citizenship application, you have to tell USCIS your new address. USCIS needs to know where to send your interview notice.

Hai's Form

Part 5. Information About Your Residence

1. Where have you lived during the last five years? Provide your most recent residence and then list every location where you have lived during the last five years. If you need extra space, use additional sheets of paper.

   A. Current Physical Address

   Street Number and Name

   3235 NORTH 58TH ST.   Apt. ☒ Ste. ☐ Flr. ☐ Number D-5

   City or Town: OAKLAND   County: ALAMEDA   State: CA   ZIP Code + 4: 94649 - 7609

   Province or Region (foreign address only)

   Postal Code (foreign address only)

   Country (foreign address only)

   Dates of Residence   From (mm/dd/yyyy) 10/22/2006   To (mm/dd/yyyy) PRESENT

What Will Hai Say?

You live at 3235 North 58th Street, right?

_____ a. No. I don't.

_____ b. 10 years in Oakland.

_____ c. Yes, 3235 North 58th Street.

Hai's Interview

EXAMINER: Now, Mr. Pham, could you tell me how long you've been at your current residence?

HAI: What do you mean?

EXAMINER: You live at 3235 North 58th Street, right?

HAI: Yes.

EXAMINER: How long have you lived there?

HAI: Since 2007, I think. . . . No—since 2006.

EXAMINER: 2006?

HAI: Yes, since 2006.

Listen to Susan

I have moved three times in the last five years. I wrote all three addresses in Part 5.

Susan's Form

Part 5. Information About Your Residence (continued)   A- | 0 | 8 | 9 | 0 | 1 | 2 | 6 | 5 | 4 |

C. Physical Address 2

Street Number and Name   Apt.   Ste.   Flr.   Number

25 Bedford Court   ☐   ☐   ☐

City or Town	County	State	ZIP Code + 4
Teaneck	Bergen	NJ	07105 - 4832

Province or Region (foreign address only)	Postal Code (foreign address only)	Country (foreign address only)
		USA

Dates of Residence   From (mm/dd/yyyy) 12/01/2013   To (mm/dd/yyyy) 06/15/2014

D. Physical Address 3

Street Number and Name   Apt.   Ste.   Flr.   Number

101 South Main St   ☐   ☐   ☐

City or Town	County	State	ZIP Code + 4
Newark	Essex	NJ	07666 - 7602

Province or Region (foreign address only)	Postal Code (foreign address only)	Country (foreign address only)
		USA

Dates of Residence   From (mm/dd/yyyy) 04/01/2012   To (mm/dd/yyyy) 12/01/2013

E. Physical Address 4

Street Number and Name   Apt.   Ste.   Flr.   Number

   ☐   ☐   ☐

City or Town	County	State	ZIP Code + 4
Kingston			-

Province or Region (foreign address only)	Postal Code (foreign address only)	Country (foreign address only)
		Jamaica

Dates of Residence   From (mm/dd/yyyy) 01/22/2011   To (mm/dd/yyyy) 03/31/2012

What Will Susan Say?

How long have you lived at your current address?

_____ a. Since June 2014.

_____ b. Yes, I did.

_____ c. Bridgeport, Connecticut.

Susan's Interview

EXAMINER: How long have you lived at your current address?

SUSAN: Since June 2014.

EXAMINER: What was your previous address?

SUSAN: Excuse me?

EXAMINER: What was your address before you lived in Bridgeport?

SUSAN: 25 Bedford Court, Teaneck, New Jersey.

EXAMINER: When did you begin living at that address?

SUSAN: In late 2013.

EXAMINER: Have you lived anywhere else in the last five years?

SUSAN: Yes. I lived in Newark, New Jersey, and before that I lived in Jamaica.

What Will You Say?

How long have you lived at your current address?
How long have you lived at this address?
How long have you lived where you are now?

What was your previous address?
What was your last address?
Where did you live before?

When did you begin living at that address?
When did you move to that address?
When did you leave that address?

Have you lived anywhere else in the last five years?
Have you lived at any other addresses?
Where else have you lived since you became a permanent resident?

Your Form

Part 5. Information About Your Residence (continued)

A- ☐☐☐☐☐☐☐☐☐

C. Physical Address 2

Street Number and Name

[   ]   Apt. ☐ Ste. ☐ Flr. ☐ Number [   ]

City or Town   County   State   ZIP Code + 4

[   ]   [   ]   [   ]   [   ] - [   ]

Province or Region   Postal Code   Country
(foreign address only)   (foreign address only)   (foreign address only)

[   ]   [   ]   [   ]

Dates of Residence   From (mm/dd/yyyy)   To (mm/dd/yyyy)

[   ]   [   ]

D. Physical Address 3

Street Number and Name

[   ]   Apt. ☐ Ste. ☐ Flr. ☐ Number [   ]

City or Town   County   State   ZIP Code + 4

[   ]   [   ]   [   ]   [   ] - [   ]

Province or Region   Postal Code   Country
(foreign address only)   (foreign address only)   (foreign address only)

[   ]   [   ]   [   ]

Dates of Residence   From (mm/dd/yyyy)   To (mm/dd/yyyy)

[   ]   [   ]

E. Physical Address 4

Street Number and Name

[   ]   Apt. ☐ Ste. ☐ Flr. ☐ Number [   ]

City or Town   County   State   ZIP Code + 4

[   ]   [   ]   [   ]   [   ] - [   ]

Province or Region   Postal Code   Country
(foreign address only)   (foreign address only)   (foreign address only)

[   ]   [   ]   [   ]

Dates of Residence   From (mm/dd/yyyy)   To (mm/dd/yyyy)

[   ]   [   ]

Information About Your Parents

Listen to Celia

 My father became a U.S. citizen many years ago, but he returned to Portugal. I was born in Portugal. After I came to America, I decided to apply for citizenship. I talked to an immigration expert about my application. He asked questions about my family and looked at my papers. Then he gave me a big surprise. He told me that I am a U.S. citizen now!

If your mother or father is (or was) a citizen, check with an immigration expert. You might be a U.S. citizen already.

Listen to Hai

My mother and father died many years ago in Vietnam. They never came to America. They were citizens of Vietnam. I did not need to fill in Part 6.

Hai's Form

Part 6. Information About Your Parents

If neither one of your parents is a United States citizen, then skip this part and go to Part 7.

What Will Hai Say?

Are either of your parents U.S. citizens?

_____ a. Yes. My mother and father.

_____ b. No. They never came to America.

_____ c. They died a long time ago.

 ## Hai's Interview

EXAMINER: Are either of your parents U.S. citizens?

HAI: No. They never came to America.

EXAMINER: So they were citizens of Vietnam?

HAI: Yes.

 ## What Will You Say?

Were your parents married before your 18th birthday?

Is your mother a U.S. citizen?
Is your father a U.S. citizen?
Are either of your parents U.S. citizens?

Your Form

<hr>

Part 6. Information About Your Parents

If neither one of your parents is a United States citizen, then skip this part and go to Part 7.

1. Were your parents married before your 18th birthday? ☐ Yes ☐ No

Information About Your Mother

2. Is your mother a U.S. citizen? ☐ Yes ☐ No

   If you answered "Yes," complete the following information. If you answered "No," go to **Item Number 3**.

<hr>

Part 6. Information About Your Parents (continued)   A- ☐☐☐☐☐☐☐☐☐

   A. Current Legal Name of U.S. Citizen Mother

   Family Name (Last Name)   Given Name (First Name)   Middle Name (if applicable)

   B. Mother's Country of Birth   C. Mother's Date of Birth (mm/dd/yyyy)

   D. Date Mother Became a U.S. Citizen   E. Mother's A-Number
       (if known) (mm/dd/yyyy)   (if any)

                                       ▶ A- ☐☐☐☐☐☐☐☐☐

Information About Your Father

3. Is your father a U.S. citizen? ☐ Yes ☐ No

   If you answered "Yes," complete the information below. If you answered "No," go to **Part 7**.

   A. Current Legal Name of U.S. Citizen Father

   Family Name (Last Name)   Given Name (First Name)   Middle Name (if applicable)

   B. Father's Country of Birth   C. Father's Date of Birth (mm/dd/yyyy)

   D. Date Father Became a U.S. Citizen   E. Father's A-Number
       (if known) (mm/dd/yyyy)   (if any)

                                       ▶ A- ☐☐☐☐☐☐☐☐☐

N-400 Part 7
Biographic Information

🔘 Listen to Hai

When you apply to become a citizen, USCIS checks your fingerprints. They need information to go with your fingerprints. You put that information in Part 7 of your application.

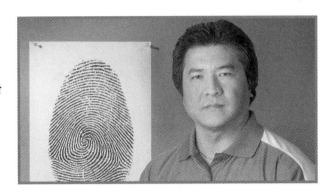

Tell whether you are Hispanic or Latino. Tell whether you are White, Asian, Black, Native American, or Native Hawaiian. Tell how tall you are and how many pounds you weigh. And tell your eye color and hair color.

These questions are on the application, but the examiner will not ask them at your interview.

Hai's Form

Part 7. Biographic Information

NOTE: USCIS requires you to complete the categories below to conduct background checks. (See the Form N-400 Instructions for more information.)

1. Ethnicity (Select **only one** box)
   - ☐ Hispanic or Latino   ☒ Not Hispanic or Latino

2. Race (Select **all applicable** boxes)
   - ☐ White   ☒ Asian   ☐ Black or African American   ☐ American Indian or Alaska Native   ☐ Native Hawaiian or Other Pacific Islander

3. Height   Feet   `5`   Inches   `8`   4. Weight   Pounds   `1` `7` `0`

5. Eye color (Select **only one** box)
   - ☐ Black   ☐ Blue   ☒ Brown   ☐ Gray   ☐ Green   ☐ Hazel   ☐ Maroon   ☐ Pink   ☐ Unknown/Other

6. Hair color (Select **only one** box)
   - ☐ Bald (No hair)   ☒ Black   ☐ Blond   ☐ Brown   ☐ Gray   ☐ Red   ☐ Sandy   ☐ White   ☐ Unknown/Other

---

Your Form

Part 7. Biographic Information

NOTE: USCIS requires you to complete the categories below to conduct background checks. (See the Form N-400 Instructions for more information.)

1. Ethnicity (Select **only one** box)

   ☐ Hispanic or Latino   ☐ Not Hispanic or Latino

2. Race (Select **all applicable** boxes)

   ☐ White   ☐ Asian   ☐ Black or African American   ☐ American Indian or Alaska Native   ☐ Native Hawaiian or Other Pacific Islander

3. Height   Feet ☐   Inches ☐   **4.** Weight   Pounds ☐ ☐ ☐

5. Eye color (Select **only one** box)

   ☐ Black   ☐ Blue   ☐ Brown   ☐ Gray   ☐ Green   ☐ Hazel   ☐ Maroon   ☐ Pink   ☐ Unknown/ Other

6. Hair color (Select **only one** box)

   ☐ Bald (No hair)   ☐ Black   ☐ Blond   ☐ Brown   ☐ Gray   ☐ Red   ☐ Sandy   ☐ White   ☐ Unknown/ Other

N-400 Part 8
Employment and Schools

Listen to Maria

I work at the Holiday Hotel in Dallas, Texas. Holiday Hotel is my employer. I've worked there since 2005.

I'm a housekeeper. This is my only job. I don't have any other jobs. I haven't worked in any other place in the U.S.

Maria's Form

Part 8. Information About Your Employment and Schools You Attended

List where you have worked or attended school full time or part time during the last five years. Provide information for the complete time period. Include all military, police, and/or intelligence service. Begin by providing information about your most recent or current employment, studies, or unemployment (if applicable). Provide the locations and dates where you worked, were self-employed, were unemployed, or have studied for the last five years. If you worked for yourself, type or print "self-employed." If you were unemployed, type or print "unemployed." If you need extra space, use additional sheets of paper.

1. Employer or School Name

Holiday Hotel

Street Number and Name | Apt. Ste. Flr. Number

125 Spring St.

City or Town | State | ZIP Code + 4

Dallas | **TX** | **75211** - **5312**

Province or Region (foreign address only) | Postal Code (foreign address only) | Country (foreign address only)

Date From (mm/dd/yyyy) | Date To (mm/dd/yyyy) | Your Occupation

09/14/2005 | **present** | **housekeeper**

What Will Maria Say?

Have you had any other jobs in the last five years?

_____ a. No.

_____ b. Since 2005.

_____ c. Holiday Hotel.

Maria's Interview

EXAMINER: Are you still working at the Holiday Hotel?

MARIA: Yes.

EXAMINER: How long have you worked there?

MARIA: How long? Uh . . . since 2005.

EXAMINER: What do you do there?

MARIA: I'm a housekeeper.

EXAMINER: Have you had any other jobs in the last five years?

MARIA: No.

Listen to Hai

I have my own store. I'm a store manager. My family bought the store in 2012. I am self-employed. I don't have a boss.

Before we bought the store, I worked in Green's Market. I was a cashier. Also, I was a gas station attendant at Springfield Arco.

Hai's Form

| **Part 8. Information About Your Employment and Schools You Attended** |

List where you have worked or attended school full time or part time during the last five years. Provide information for the complete time period. Include all military, police, and/or intelligence service. Begin by providing information about your most recent or current employment, studies, or unemployment (if applicable). Provide the locations and dates where you worked, were self-employed, were unemployed, or have studied for the last five years. If you worked for yourself, type or print "self-employed." If you were unemployed, type or print "unemployed." If you need extra space, use additional sheets of paper.

1. Employer or School Name

SELF-EMPLOYED - ASIAN AMERICAN MARKET

Street Number and Name — Apt. Ste. Flr. Number

2123 NORTH 16TH ST.

City or Town — State — ZIP Code + 4

OAKLAND — CA — 94577 - 8520

Province or Region (foreign address only) — Postal Code (foreign address only) — Country (foreign address only)

Date From (mm/dd/yyyy) — Date To (mm/dd/yyyy) — Your Occupation

05/01/2012 — PRESENT — MANAGER

2. Employer or School Name

GREEN'S MARKET

Street Number and Name — Apt. Ste. Flr. Number

43 MAIN ST.

City or Town — State — ZIP Code + 4

OAKLAND — CA — 94577 - 4398

Province or Region (foreign address only) — Postal Code (foreign address only) — Country (foreign address only)

Date From (mm/dd/yyyy) — Date To (mm/dd/yyyy) — Your Occupation

12/03/2009 — 04/28/2012 — CASHIER

3. Employer or School Name

SPRINGFIELD ARCO

Street Number and Name

515 MAIN ST.

Apt. ☐ Ste. ☐ Flr. ☐ Number ☐

City or Town

OAKLAND

State: CA   ZIP Code + 4: 94577 - 6497

Province or Region
(foreign address only)

Postal Code
(foreign address only)

Country
(foreign address only)

Date From (mm/dd/yyyy): 01/27/2011   Date To (mm/dd/yyyy): 03/18/2012   Your Occupation: GAS STATION ATTENDANT

What Will Hai Say?

Who is your current employer?

_____ a. No, I don't.

_____ b. We sell food.

_____ c. I'm self-employed.

Hai's Interview

EXAMINER: What is your occupation?

HAI: I'm a store manager.

EXAMINER: Who is your current employer?

HAI: I'm self-employed.

EXAMINER: So you work for yourself?

HAI: Yes, that's right. My family owns a store.

EXAMINER: How long have you been managing the store?

HAI: Since 2012. Before that, I was a cashier at Green's Market.

EXAMINER: When did you begin that job?

HAI: Let me think. . . . I think that was in 2009.

EXAMINER: Have you worked anywhere else since you came to America?

HAI: Yes. I worked at a gas station for a couple of years.

EXAMINER: What was the name of the gas station?

HAI: Springfield Arco.

EXAMINER: And do you remember the dates that you worked there?

HAI: I'm sorry. It's hard to remember. I think it was around 2011.

Listen to Otto

 I'm retired. I don't work anymore. I stopped working nine years ago. Now I stay at home. I also spend a lot of time in the park.

Otto's Form

Part 8. Information About Your Employment and Schools You Attended

List where you have worked or attended school full time or part time during the last five years. Provide information for the complete time period. Include all military, police, and/or intelligence service. Begin by providing information about your most recent or current employment, studies, or unemployment (if applicable). Provide the locations and dates where you worked, were self-employed, were unemployed, or have studied for the last five years. If you worked for yourself, type or print "self-employed." If you were unemployed, type or print "unemployed." If you need extra space, use additional sheets of paper.

1. Employer or School Name

   `retired`

   Street Number and Name | Apt. ☐ Ste. ☐ Flr. ☐ Number

   `N/A`

   City or Town | State | ZIP Code + 4

   Province or Region (foreign address only) | Postal Code (foreign address only) | Country (foreign address only)

   Date From (mm/dd/yyyy) | Date To (mm/dd/yyyy) | Your Occupation

   `05/01/2007` | | `N/A`

What Will Otto Say?

Have you been employed in the last five years?

_____ a. Yes, I stay home.

_____ b. No. I don't work anymore.

_____ c. Nine years ago.

Otto's Interview

EXAMINER: Have you been employed in the last five years?

OTTO: Employed?

EXAMINER: Have you worked? Did you have a job?

OTTO: No. I don't work anymore.

EXAMINER: You're retired?

OTTO: Yes. Retired.

EXAMINER: How long have you been retired?

OTTO: Nine years.

Listen to Chong

I just got a job in a restaurant. I'm a waitress.

Before that, I didn't work. I went to English classes, and I stayed home with my children.

Chong's Form

| Part 8. Information About Your Employment and Schools You Attended | A- 0 9 8 7 6 5 4 3 2 |

List where you have worked or attended school full time or part time during the last five years. Provide information for the complete time period. Include all military, police, and/or intelligence service. Begin by providing information about your most recent or current employment, studies, or unemployment (if applicable). Provide the locations and dates where you worked, were self-employed, were unemployed, or have studied for the last five years. If you worked for yourself, type or print "self-employed." If you were unemployed, type or print "unemployed." If you need extra space, use additional sheets of paper.

1. Employer or School Name

Lucys Diner

Street Number and Name   Apt. Ste. Flr. Number

45 Maple St   ☐ ☐ ☐

City or Town   State   ZIP Code + 4

Edmonds   WA   98026 - 3408

Province or Region (foreign address only)   Postal Code (foreign address only)   Country (foreign address only)

   USA

Date From (mm/dd/yyyy)   Date To (mm/dd/yyyy)   Your Occupation

06/09/2013   present   Food Preparation and Service

2. Employer or School Name

Edmonds Adult School

Street Number and Name   Apt. Ste. Flr. Number

42 Main St   ☐ ☐ ☐

City or Town   State   ZIP Code + 4

Edmonds   WA   98026 - 7757

Province or Region (foreign address only)   Postal Code (foreign address only)   Country (foreign address only)

   USA

Date From (mm/dd/yyyy)   Date To (mm/dd/yyyy)   Your Occupation

03/12/2009   11/20/2012

What Will Chong Say?

What do you do at Lucy's Diner?

_____ a. I'm on welfare.

_____ b. I'm a waitress.

_____ c. Yes, it's my job.

 ## Chong's Interview

EXAMINER: Are you currently employed?

CHONG: You mean . . . working?

EXAMINER: Yes. Do you have a job?

CHONG: Yes. I work at Lucy's Diner.

EXAMINER: What is your position there?

CHONG: Position?

EXAMINER: Your occupation, your job. What do you do at Lucy's Diner?

CHONG: Oh. I'm a waitress.

EXAMINER: What did you do before that?

CHONG: I didn't have a job. I stayed home to take care of my children. And I went to English classes.

EXAMINER: How did you support yourself?

CHONG: Support?

EXAMINER: How did you get money to pay the rent? Buy food?

CHONG: Oh. I was on welfare. And my ex-husband paid child support.

What Will You Say?

Do you work?
Do you have a job right now?
Are you currently employed?
Are you currently working?

Who is your current employer?
Where do you work?
What is your employer's address?

How long have you worked there?
When did you begin working there?
How long have you been working there?
How long have you had that job?

What do you do there?
What kind of work do you do?
What is your position?
What job do you have there?
What is your occupation?

Where did you work before that?
What did you do?
When did you leave that job?
How long did you work there?

Have you had any other jobs?
Have you worked anywhere else in the last five years?
Where else have you worked since you became a permanent resident?

Your Form

Part 8. Information About Your Employment and Schools You Attended

List where you have worked or attended school full time or part time during the last five years. Provide information for the complete time period. Include all military, police, and/or intelligence service. Begin by providing information about your most recent or current employment, studies, or unemployment (if applicable). Provide the locations and dates where you worked, were self-employed, were unemployed, or have studied for the last five years. If you worked for yourself, type or print "self-employed." If you were unemployed, type or print "unemployed." If you need extra space, use additional sheets of paper.

1. Employer or School Name

Street Number and Name   Apt.   Ste.   Flr.   Number

City or Town   State   ZIP Code + 4

Province or Region
(foreign address only)   Postal Code
(foreign address only)   Country
(foreign address only)

Date From (mm/dd/yyyy)   Date To (mm/dd/yyyy)   Your Occupation

2. Employer or School Name

Street Number and Name   Apt.   Ste.   Flr.   Number

City or Town   State   ZIP Code + 4

Province or Region
(foreign address only)   Postal Code
(foreign address only)   Country
(foreign address only)

Date From (mm/dd/yyyy)   Date To (mm/dd/yyyy)   Your Occupation

3. Employer or School Name

Street Number and Name   Apt.   Ste.   Flr.   Number

City or Town   State   ZIP Code + 4

Province or Region
(foreign address only)   Postal Code
(foreign address only)   Country
(foreign address only)

Date From (mm/dd/yyyy)   Date To (mm/dd/yyyy)   Your Occupation

N-400 Part 9
Time Outside the United States

 Listen to Hai

 After I came to America, I stayed here. I did not leave America.

I did not take any trips outside this country.

Hai's Form

Part 9. Time Outside the United States		
1.	How many **total days (24 hours or longer)** did you spend outside the United States during the last 5 years?	0 days
2.	How many trips of **24 hours or longer** have you taken outside the United States during the last 5 years?	0 trips

What Will Hai Say?

Have you left the United States since you became a permanent resident?

_____ a. July 8, 2003.

_____ b. No.

_____ c. Yes, Vietnam.

 Hai's Interview

EXAMINER: Have you left the United States since you became a permanent resident?

HAI: I'm sorry. I didn't hear. Can you say that again?

EXAMINER: Have you left the U.S.? Have you gone to any other countries?

HAI: Other country? No.

EXAMINER: You haven't visited your family in Vietnam?

HAI: No. I stay here.

Listen to Maria

I go to Mexico every year to see my mother. I stay with her for two weeks. Then I come home.

I can not remember exactly which dates I stayed in Mexico. I copied the dates from my passport onto my citizenship form.

Maria's Form

Part 9. Time Outside the United States

1. How many **total days (24 hours or longer)** did you spend outside the United States during the last 5 years? | 87 | days

2. How many trips of **24 hours or longer** have you taken outside the United States during the last 5 years? | 5 | trips

3. List below all the trips of **24 hours or longer** that you have taken outside the United States during the last 5 years. Start with your most recent trip and work backwards. If you need extra space, use additional sheets of paper.

Date You Left the United States (mm/dd/yyyy)	Date You Returned to the United States (mm/dd/yyyy)	Did Trip Last 6 Months or More?	Countries to Which You Traveled	Total Days Outside the United States
02/20/2016	03/10/2016	☐ Yes ☑ No	Mexico	18
12/02/2015	12/14/2015	☐ Yes ☑ No	Mexico	12
03/15/2014	03/30/2014	☐ Yes ☑ No	Mexico	15
11/18/2013	12/18/2013	☐ Yes ☑ No	Mexico	30
02/01/2012	02/13/2012	☐ Yes ☑ No	Mexico	12
		☐ Yes ☐ No		

What Will Maria Say?

How long did you stay in Mexico?

_____ a. No, I didn't.

_____ b. Last year.

_____ c. Two weeks.

 ## Maria's Interview

EXAMINER: Have you spent any time outside the U.S. since you became a permanent resident?

MARIA: No . . . ?

EXAMINER: Are you sure?

MARIA: Uh . . . I went to Mexico many times.

EXAMINER: How long did you stay in Mexico?

MARIA: Two weeks. I stay two weeks, then I come back, every year.

Listen to Chong

 I have been outside the U.S. one time since I came here. My family went to Canada for vacation in 2013. We left on July 14, and we returned on July 29. We were away for two weeks.

Chong's Form

| Part 9. Time Outside the United States | A- 0 9 8 7 6 5 4 3 2 |

1. How many **total days (24 hours or longer)** did you spend outside the United States during the last 5 years? | 15 | days

2. How many trips of **24 hours or longer** have you taken outside the United States during the last 5 years? | 1 | trips

3. List below all the trips of **24 hours or longer** that you have taken outside the United States during the last 5 years. Start with your most recent trip and work backwards. If you need extra space, use additional sheets of paper.

Date You Left the United States (mm/dd/yyyy)	Date You Returned to the United States (mm/dd/yyyy)	Did Trip Last 6 Months or More?	Countries to Which You Traveled	Total Days Outside the United States
07/14/2013	07/29/2013	☐ Yes ☒ No	Canada	15
		☐ Yes ☐ No		

What Will Chong Say?

How long did you stay in Canada?

_____ a. Two weeks.

_____ b. For vacation.

_____ c. July 14.

 ## Chong's Interview

EXAMINER: Have you been outside the U.S. in the last five years?

CHONG: Yes. One time.

EXAMINER: Where did you go?

CHONG: Canada.

EXAMINER: How long did you stay in Canada?

CHONG: Two weeks.

EXAMINER: Do you remember when that was?

CHONG: Yes. It was in July . . . uh, 2013.

◉ Listen to Sergei

My father died in 2013. I went to Russia for my father's funeral. I stayed from January 12 to February 20.

I went back to Russia another time for my brother's wedding. He got married in June 2015. I stayed from June 1 to June 25.

I was absent from the U.S. two times since I became a permanent resident. Both times I went to Russia.

Sergei's Form

Part 9. Time Outside the United States

1. How many **total days (24 hours or longer)** did you spend outside the United States during the last 5 years? | **64** | days

2. How many trips of **24 hours or longer** have you taken outside the United States during the last 5 years? | **2** | trips

3. List below all the trips of **24 hours or longer** that you have taken outside the United States during the last 5 years. Start with your most recent trip and work backwards. If you need extra space, use additional sheets of paper.

Date You Left the United States (mm/dd/yyyy)	Date You Returned to the United States (mm/dd/yyyy)	Did Trip Last 6 Months or More?	Countries to Which You Traveled	Total Days Outside the United States
06/01/2015	06/25/2015	☐ Yes ☒ No	Russia	25
01/12/2013	02/20/2013	☐ Yes ☒ No	Russia	39
		☐ Yes ☐ No		
		☐ Yes ☐ No		
		☐ Yes ☐ No		
		☐ Yes ☐ No		

What Will Sergei Say?

Have you taken any trips in the last five years?

_____ a. No, that's all.

_____ b. Yes. Two trips.

_____ c. For a wedding.

Sergei's Interview

EXAMINER: It says here that you've made two trips out of the country during the last five years.

SERGEI: Yes.

EXAMINER: Both to Russia, is that right?

SERGEI: Yes. In 2013 and 2015.

EXAMINER: Have you taken any other trips in the last five years?

SERGEI: You mean . . . more trips?

EXAMINER: Yes.

SERGEI: No. No more trips.

 ## What Will You Say?

Have you taken any trips outside the U.S. during the last five years?
Have you left the United States since you came here?
Have you ever left the country?
Have you traveled outside the country in the last five years?

How many times did you go outside the U.S.?
How many trips have you taken outside the U.S.?

When did you leave the U.S.?
When did you return?

How long were you gone?
How many days were you outside the U.S.?
For how long were you away?
How long was your trip?

Did you stay outside of the U.S. for six months?

Where did you go?
Which country did you visit?

Have you been outside the U.S. any other times?
Have you taken any trips since then?
Did you take any other trips outside the U.S.?

Your Form

Part 9. Time Outside the United States

1. How many **total days (24 hours or longer)** did you spend outside the United States during the last 5 years? [   ] days

2. How many trips of **24 hours or longer** have you taken outside the United States during the last 5 years? [   ] trips

3. List below all the trips of **24 hours or longer** that you have taken outside the United States during the last 5 years. Start with your most recent trip and work backwards. If you need extra space, use additional sheets of paper.

Date You Left the United States (mm/dd/yyyy)	Date You Returned to the United States (mm/dd/yyyy)	Did Trip Last 6 Months or More?	Countries to Which You Traveled	Total Days Outside the United States
		☐ Yes ☐ No		
		☐ Yes ☐ No		
		☐ Yes ☐ No		
		☐ Yes ☐ No		
		☐ Yes ☐ No		
		☐ Yes ☐ No		

N-400 Part 10
Information About Your Marital History

Single

 ### Listen to Hai

 I'm single. I have never been married. I don't have anything to write in Part 10.

Hai's Form

Part 10. Information About Your Marital History

1.   What is your current marital status?

☒ Single, Never Married ☐ Married ☐ Divorced ☐ Widowed ☐ Separated ☐ Marriage Annulled

If you are single and have **never** married, go to **Part 11.**

What Will Hai Say?

Have you ever been married before?

_____ a. No.

_____ b. Yes, single.

_____ c. My wife.

 ## Hai's Interview

EXAMINER: Are you married?

HAI: Married? No.

EXAMINER: Have you ever been married before?

HAI: No. Never.

Listen to Chong

I got married when I was very young. But my husband and I were not happy together. We decided to get a divorce. I am not married anymore. I am divorced.

Chong's Form

Part 10. Information About Your Marital History

1. What is your current marital status?

☐ Single, Never Married   ☐ Married   ☒ Divorced   ☐ Widowed   ☐ Separated   ☐ Marriage Annulled

If you are single and have **never** married, go to **Part 11.**

2. If you are married, is your spouse a current member of the U.S. armed forces?   ☐ Yes   ☐ No

3. How many times have you been married (including annulled marriages, marriages to other people, and marriages to the same person)?   1

9. If you were married before, provide the following information about your prior spouse. If you have more than one previous marriage, provide that information on additional sheets of paper.

A. My Prior Spouse's Legal Name

Family Name (Last Name)	Given Name (First Name)	Middle Name (if applicable)
Barton	Peter	Todd

B. My Prior Spouse's Immigration Status When My Marriage Ended (if known)

☒ U.S. Citizen   ☐ Lawful Permanent Resident   ☐ Other (Explain):

C. My Prior Spouse's Date of Birth (mm/dd/yyyy)
01/02/1978

D. My Prior Spouse's Country of Birth
USA

E. My Prior Spouse's Country of Citizenship or Nationality
USA

F. Date of Marriage with My Prior Spouse (mm/dd/yyyy)
04/06/1998

G. Date Marriage Ended with My Prior Spouse (mm/dd/yyyy)
05/12/2007

H. How Marriage Ended with My Prior Spouse
☐ Annulled   ☒ Divorced   ☐ Spouse Deceased   ☐ Other (Explain):

What Will Chong Say?

You're divorced, right?

_____ a. No, I'm not married.

_____ b. Ten years ago.

_____ c. Yes, I'm divorced.

◉ Chong's Interview

EXAMINER: You're divorced, right?

CHONG: Yes, I'm divorced.

EXAMINER: Can you tell me the name of your prior spouse?

CHONG: I don't understand.

EXAMINER: Your ex-husband. What was his name?

CHONG: Peter Todd Barton.

EXAMINER: What is his immigration status—is he a U.S. citizen?

CHONG: Yes.

EXAMINER: Do you know his date of birth?

CHONG: Yes. January 2nd, 1978.

EXAMINER: When did you marry him?

CHONG: April 6th, 1998

EXAMINER: And you were divorced—when?

CHONG: In 2007.

Information About Your Spouse

 Listen to Susan

 In my life I have had just one husband. My husband's name is Jean Claud Santos.

He was born on March 10, 1986. March 10, 1986, is his date of birth.

We got married on June 12, 2009. June 12, 2009, is our date of marriage.

My husband lives with me. His address and my address are the same.

Jean Claud is not a member of the armed forces.

He works at East Country Motors.

Susan's Form

<table>
<tr><td colspan="3">Part 10. Information About Your Marital History</td></tr>
</table>

1. What is your current marital status?

☐ Single, Never Married   ☒ Married   ☐ Divorced   ☐ Widowed   ☐ Separated   ☐ Marriage Annulled

If you are single and have **never** married, go to **Part 11.**

2. If you are married, is your spouse a current member of the U.S. armed forces?   ☐ Yes   ☒ No

3. How many times have you been married (including annulled marriages, marriages to other people, and marriages to the same person)?   `1`

4. If you are married now, provide the following information about your current spouse.

A. Current Spouse's Legal Name

Family Name (Last Name)	Given Name (First Name)	Middle Name (if applicable)
Santos	Jean	Claud

B. Current Spouse's Previous Legal Name

Family Name (Last Name)	Given Name (First Name)	Middle Name (if applicable)
NA		

C. Other Names Used by Current Spouse (include nicknames, aliases, and maiden name, if applicable)

Family Name (Last Name)	Given Name (First Name)	Middle Name (if applicable)
NA		

D. Current Spouse's Date of Birth (mm/dd/yyyy)   **E.** Date You Entered into Marriage with Current Spouse (mm/dd/yyyy)

03/10/1986	06/12/2009

What Will Susan Say?

You have a husband now, is that right?

_____ a. Yes.

_____ b. In 2009.

_____ c. He's at work now.

⊚ Susan's Interview

EXAMINER: How many times have you been married?

SUSAN: I got married in 2009.

EXAMINER: I'm asking you how many times.

SUSAN: I don't understand.

EXAMINER: Did you ever have a different husband before Jean Claud?

SUSAN: No. Jean Claud is the only one.

Susan's Form

Part 10. Information About Your Marital History (continued)	A-	0 8 9 0 1 2 6 5 4

F. Current Spouse's Present Home Address

Street Number and Name

`with me`

Apt. ☐ Ste. ☐ Flr. ☐ Number ☐

City or Town | County | State | ZIP Code + 4

Province or Region (foreign address only) | Postal Code (foreign address only) | Country (foreign address only)

G. Current Spouse's Current Employer or Company

`East Country Motors`

5. Is your current spouse a U.S. citizen? ☒ Yes ☐ No

If you answered "Yes," answer **Item Number 6.** If you answered "No," go to **Item Number 7.**

6. If your current spouse is a U.S. citizen, complete the following information.

A. When did your current spouse become a U.S. citizen?

☐ At Birth - Go to **Item Number 8.** ☒ Other - Complete the following information.

B. Date Your Current Spouse Became a U.S. Citizen (mm/dd/yyyy)

`01/16/2008`

Listen to Susan

My husband was born in Haiti, but he's a U.S. citizen now. He became a citizen on January 16, 2008.

What Will Susan Say?

Your husband is a U.S. citizen, is that correct?

_____ a. Yes. I want to be a citizen.

_____ b. Yes. He is a citizen.

_____ c. Yes. I have a husband.

Susan's Interview

EXAMINER: Your husband is a U.S. citizen, is that correct?

SUSAN: Yes. He is a citizen.

EXAMINER: Do you know when he became a citizen? What date was it?

SUSAN: I don't remember the date exactly. But the year was 2008.

Listen to Nick

My wife is not a U.S. citizen. She is a permanent resident. She is also from Cambodia, like me.

Nick's Form

5. Is your current spouse a U.S. citizen? ☐ Yes ☒ No

   If you answered "Yes," answer **Item Number 6.** If you answered "No," go to **Item Number 7.**

7. If your current spouse is not a U.S. citizen, complete the following information.

   A. Current Spouse's Country of Citizenship or Nationality   B. Current Spouse's A-Number (if any)

   | Cambodia |

   ▶ A- | 2 | 2 | 3 | 0 | 0 | 0 | 0 | 9 | 3 |

   C. Current Spouse's Immigration Status

   ☒ Lawful Permanent Resident   ☐ Other (Explain): | |

What Will Nick Say?

Is your wife a U.S. citizen?

_____ a. I'm married.

_____ b. No. She has a green card.

_____ c. After three years.

Nick's Interview

EXAMINER: Is your wife a citizen of the United States?

NICK: Excuse me. You ask about my wife, right?

EXAMINER: Yes. Is she a U.S. citizen?

NICK: No. She has a green card.

EXAMINER: So she's a permanent resident.

NICK: Yes.

Listen to Maria

My husband's name was José Maria Perez. We were married on June 16, 1970.

José was a permanent resident. He died August 1, 2010. I am a widow.

Maria's Form

Part 10. Information About Your Marital History

1. What is your current marital status?

☐ Single, Never Married ☐ Married ☐ Divorced ☑ Widowed ☐ Separated ☐ Marriage Annulled

If you are single and have **never** married, go to **Part 11**.

2. If you are married, is your spouse a current member of the U.S. armed forces? ☐ Yes ☐ No

3. How many times have you been married (including annulled marriages, marriages to other people, and marriages to the same person)? [1]

9. If you were married before, provide the following information about your prior spouse. If you have more than one previous marriage, provide that information on additional sheets of paper.

A. My Prior Spouse's Legal Name

Family Name (Last Name)	Given Name (First Name)	Middle Name (if applicable)
Perez	José	Maria

B. My Prior Spouse's Immigration Status When My Marriage Ended (if known)

☐ U.S. Citizen ☑ Lawful Permanent Resident ☐ Other (Explain): [   ]

C. My Prior Spouse's Date of Birth (mm/dd/yyyy)   **D.** My Prior Spouse's Country of Birth

03/14/1952	Mexico

E. My Prior Spouse's Country of Citizenship or Nationality   **F.** Date of Marriage with My Prior Spouse (mm/dd/yyyy)

Mexico	06/16/1970

G. Date Marriage Ended with My Prior Spouse (mm/dd/yyyy)

08/01/2010

H. How Marriage Ended with My Prior Spouse

☐ Annulled ☐ Divorced ☑ Spouse Deceased ☐ Other (Explain): [   ]

What Will Maria Say?

Was your husband a U.S. citizen?

_____ a. No. He died in 2010.

_____ b. No. He was a permanent resident.

_____ c. Only one time.

 Maria's Interview

EXAMINER: How many times have you been married?

MARIA: Only one time.

EXAMINER: And you got married in 2010, right?

MARIA: No, in 1970. 2010 was the year my husband died.

EXAMINER: Was your husband a U.S. citizen?

MARIA: No. He was a permanent resident.

Listen to Susan

My husband was divorced before he married me.

A long time ago, he had a different wife, Marianne. Marianne is his former wife. She is his previous wife.

Susan's Form

8. How many times has your current spouse been married (including annulled marriages, marriages to other people, and marriages to the same person)? If your current spouse has been married before, provide the following information about your current spouse's prior spouse.

   | 2 |

   If your current spouse has had more than one previous marriage, provide that information on additional sheets of paper.

   A. Legal Name of My Current Spouse's Prior Spouse

Family Name (Last Name)	Given Name (First Name)	Middle Name (if applicable)
Santos	Marianne	N/A

   B. Immigration Status of My Current Spouse's Prior Spouse (if known)

   ☐ U.S. Citizen   ☐ Lawful Permanent Resident   ☒ Other (Explain): citizen of Haiti

   C. Date of Birth of My Current Spouse's Prior Spouse (mm/dd/yyyy)

   12/12/1987

   D. Country of Birth of My Current Spouse's Prior Spouse

   Haiti

   E. Country of Citizenship or Nationality of My Current Spouse's Prior Spouse

   Haiti

Part 10. Information About Your Marital History (continued)   A- 0 8 9 0 1 2 6 5 4

   F. My Current Spouse's Date of Marriage with Prior Spouse (mm/dd/yyyy)

   11/01/2004

   G. Date My Current Spouse's Marriage Ended with Prior Spouse (mm/dd/yyyy)

   02/28/2006

   H. How My Current Spouse's Marriage Ended with Prior Spouse

   ☐ Annulled   ☒ Divorced   ☐ Spouse Deceased   ☐ Other (Explain):

What Will Susan Say?

Do you know the date of your husband's divorce?

_____ a. Yes, he is divorced.

_____ b. It means not married anymore.

_____ c. It was in '06, I think.

🔘 Susan's Interview

EXAMINER: Tell me about your husband. Has he ever been married before?

SUSAN: Yes. He got divorced.

EXAMINER: Do you know when that happened?

SUSAN: Excuse me . . . can you ask the question again?

EXAMINER: Do you know the date of your husband's divorce?

SUSAN: I don't remember exactly. In 2006, I guess.

EXAMINER: And his former wife . . . was she a permanent resident?

SUSAN: No. They were married in Haiti. She never lived in America.

⊙ What Will You Say?

What is your marital status?
Are you married?
Are you currently married?
Have you ever been married?
How many times have you been married?

When were you married?
What was the date of your marriage?

Is this your first marriage?
Were you ever married before this?
Have you had any previous marriages?

Questions About a Husband or Former Husband

- What's your spouse's name?
- Has he ever used any other names?
- What's his date of birth?
- Was he born in the U.S.?

- Is he a member of the Armed Forces?
- Is he currently in the military?
- Where does he work?
- Who is his employer?

- Does he live with you?
- Where does he live?

- What is his immigration status?
- Is he a U.S. citizen?
- Is he a permanent resident?
- When did he become a citizen?

- How many times has he been married?
- Has he ever been married before this?
- Has he had any previous marriages?
- Does he have a former spouse?

- Do you have any former marriages?
- Do you have any prior spouses?

Questions About a Wife or Former Wife

- What's your spouse's name?
- Has she ever used any other names?
- What's her date of birth?
- Was she born in the U.S.?

- Is she a member of the Armed Forces?
- Is she currently in the military?
- Where does she work?
- Who is her employer?

- Does she live with you?
- Where does she live?

- What is her immigration status?
- Is she a U.S. citizen?
- Is she a permanent resident?
- When did she become a citizen?

- How many times has she been married?
- Has she ever been married before this?
- Has she had any previous marriages?
- Does she have a former spouse?

- Do you have any former marriages?
- Do you have any previous spouses?

Your Form

Part 10. Information About Your Marital History

1. What is your current marital status?

   ☐ Single, Never Married ☐ Married ☐ Divorced ☐ Widowed ☐ Separated ☐ Marriage Annulled

   If you are single and have **never** married, go to **Part 11**.

2. If you are married, is your spouse a current member of the U.S. armed forces? ☐ Yes ☐ No

3. How many times have you been married (including annulled marriages, marriages to other people, and marriages to the same person)?

4. If you are married now, provide the following information about your current spouse.

   A. Current Spouse's Legal Name

Family Name (Last Name)	Given Name (First Name)	Middle Name (if applicable)

   B. Current Spouse's Previous Legal Name

Family Name (Last Name)	Given Name (First Name)	Middle Name (if applicable)

   C. Other Names Used by Current Spouse (include nicknames, aliases, and maiden name, if applicable)

Family Name (Last Name)	Given Name (First Name)	Middle Name (if applicable)

   D. Current Spouse's Date of Birth (mm/dd/yyyy)

   E. Date You Entered into Marriage with Current Spouse (mm/dd/yyyy)

Part 10. Information About Your Marital History (continued)   A-[ ][ ][ ][ ][ ][ ][ ][ ][ ]

F. Current Spouse's Present Home Address

Street Number and Name   Apt. Ste. Flr. Number

[   ]   ☐   ☐   ☐   [   ]

City or Town   County   State   ZIP Code + 4

[   ]   [   ]   [   ]   [   ] - [   ]

Province or Region   Postal Code   Country
(foreign address only)   (foreign address only)   (foreign address only)

[   ]   [   ]   [   ]

G. Current Spouse's Current Employer or Company

[   ]

5. Is your current spouse a U.S. citizen?   ☐ Yes   ☐ No

If you answered "Yes," answer **Item Number 6.** If you answered "No," go to **Item Number 7.**

6. If your current spouse is a U.S. citizen, complete the following information.

  A. When did your current spouse become a U.S. citizen?

  ☐ At Birth - Go to **Item Number 8.**   ☐ Other - Complete the following information.

  B. Date Your Current Spouse Became
  a U.S. Citizen (mm/dd/yyyy)

  [   ]

7. If your current spouse is not a U.S. citizen, complete the following information.

  A. Current Spouse's Country of Citizenship or Nationality   **B.** Current Spouse's A-Number (if any)

  [   ]   ▶ A-[ ][ ][ ][ ][ ][ ][ ][ ][ ]

  C. Current Spouse's Immigration Status

  ☐ Lawful Permanent Resident   ☐ Other (Explain): [   ]

8. How many times has your current spouse been married (including annulled marriages, marriages to   [   ]
other people, and marriages to the same person)? If your current spouse has been married before,
provide the following information about your current spouse's prior spouse.

If your current spouse has had more than one previous marriage, provide that information on additional sheets of paper.

  A. Legal Name of My Current Spouse's Prior Spouse

  Family Name (Last Name)   Given Name (First Name)   Middle Name (if applicable)

  [   ]   [   ]   [   ]

  B. Immigration Status of My Current Spouse's Prior Spouse (if known)

  ☐ U.S. Citizen   ☐ Lawful Permanent Resident   ☐ Other (Explain): [   ]

  C. Date of Birth of My Current Spouse's   **D.** Country of Birth of My Current Spouse's
  Prior Spouse (mm/dd/yyyy)   Prior Spouse

  [   ]   [   ]

  E. Country of Citizenship or Nationality of My Current
  Spouse's Prior Spouse

  [   ]

Part 10. Information About Your Marital History (continued)   A- [ ][ ][ ][ ][ ][ ][ ][ ][ ]

    F. My Current Spouse's Date of Marriage   **G.** Date My Current Spouse's Marriage Ended
        with Prior Spouse (mm/dd/yyyy)   with Prior Spouse (mm/dd/yyyy)

      [_____]   [_____]

    H. How My Current Spouse's Marriage Ended with Prior Spouse

      ☐ Annulled   ☐ Divorced   ☐ Spouse Deceased   ☐ Other (Explain): [_____]

9. If you were married before, provide the following information about your prior spouse. If you have more than one previous marriage, provide that information on additional sheets of paper.

    A. My Prior Spouse's Legal Name

Family Name (Last Name)	Given Name (First Name)	Middle Name (if applicable)
[_____]	[_____]	[_____]

    B. My Prior Spouse's Immigration Status When My Marriage Ended (if known)

      ☐ U.S. Citizen   ☐ Lawful Permanent Resident   ☐ Other (Explain): [_____]

    C. My Prior Spouse's Date of Birth   **D.** My Prior Spouse's Country
        (mm/dd/yyyy)   of Birth

      [_____]   [_____]

    E. My Prior Spouse's Country of   **F.** Date of Marriage with My Prior
        Citizenship or Nationality   Spouse (mm/dd/yyyy)

      [_____]   [_____]

    G. Date Marriage Ended with My
        Prior Spouse (mm/dd/yyyy)

      [_____]

    H. How Marriage Ended with My Prior Spouse

      ☐ Annulled   ☐ Divorced   ☐ Spouse Deceased   ☐ Other (Explain): [_____]

N-400 Part 11
Information About Your Children

Listen to Hai

 I don't have any children. I've never had any children.

Hai's Form

> ### Part 11. Information About Your Children
>
> 1. Indicate your total number of children. (You must indicate **ALL** children, including: children who are alive, missing, or deceased; children born in the United States or in other countries; children under 18 years of age or older; children who are currently married or unmarried; children living with you or elsewhere; current stepchildren; legally adopted children; **and** children born when you were not married.)   `0`
>
> 2. Provide the following information about all your children (sons and daughters) listed in **Item Number 1.**, regardless of age. To list any additional children, use additional sheets of paper.
>
>   **A. Child 1**
>
>   Current Legal Name
>
> | Family Name (Last Name) | Given Name (First Name) | Middle Name (if applicable) |
> |---|---|---|
> | N/A | | |
>
> | A-Number (if any) | Date of Birth (mm/dd/yyyy) | Country of Birth |
> |---|---|---|
> | ▶ A- | | |

What Will Hai Say?

You don't have any children, do you?

_____ a. Yes.

_____ b. No.

_____ c. My family.

Hai's Interview

EXAMINER: You don't have any children, do you?

HAI: No. No children.

Listen to Chong

I have two children, Amy and Tom. My daughter Amy was born in South Korea in 1999. South Korea is her country of birth.

My son Tom was born in the U.S. Tom is a U.S. citizen. He doesn't have an A-Number.

My children live with me. Amy and Tom are my biological children. I gave birth to them. They are not my stepchildren. They are not adopted.

Chong's Form

Part 11. Information About Your Children

1. Indicate your total number of children. (You must indicate **ALL** children, including: children who are alive, missing, or deceased; children born in the United States or in other countries; children under 18 years of age or older; children who are currently married or unmarried; children living with you or elsewhere; current stepchildren; legally adopted children; **and** children born when you were not married.) | 2 |

2. Provide the following information about all your children (sons and daughters) listed in **Item Number 1.**, regardless of age. To list any additional children, use additional sheets of paper.

A. **Child 1**

Current Legal Name

Family Name (Last Name)	Given Name (First Name)	Middle Name (if applicable)
Barton	Amy	N/A

A-Number (if any)   Date of Birth (mm/dd/yyyy)   Country of Birth

▶ A- | 3 | 2 | 6 | 6 | 6 | 7 | 8 | 8 | 8 | | 01/14/1999 | | South Korea |

Part 11. Information About Your Children (continued)

A- `0` `9` `8` `7` `6` `5` `4` `3` `2`

Current Address

Street Number and Name

`with me`

Apt. ☐ Ste. ☐ Flr. ☐ Number ___

City or Town ___ County ___ State ___ ZIP Code + 4 ___ - ___

Province or Region (foreign address only) ___

Postal Code (foreign address only) ___

Country (foreign address only) ___

What is your child's relationship to you? (for example, biological child, stepchild, legally adopted child)

`biological child`

B. Child 2

Current Legal Name

Family Name (Last Name)	Given Name (First Name)	Middle Name (if applicable)
`Barton`	`Tom`	`N/A`

A-Number (if any)

▶ A- ___

Date of Birth (mm/dd/yyyy) `04/08/2001`

Country of Birth `United States`

Current Address

Street Number and Name

`with me`

Apt. ☐ Ste. ☐ Flr. ☐ Number ___

City or Town ___ County ___ State ___ ZIP Code + 4 ___ - ___

Province or Region (foreign address only) ___

Postal Code (foreign address only) ___

Country (foreign address only) ___

What is your child's relationship to you? (for example, biological child, stepchild, legally adopted child)

`biological child`

What Will Chong Say?

Where do your children live? Are they both with you?

_____ a. Yes, with me.

_____ b. No, one was born in South Korea.

_____ c. My children are citizens.

Chong's Interview

EXAMINER: How many children do you have?

CHONG: Two.

EXAMINER: And they were born in the United States?

CHONG: My daughter was born in South Korea. My son was born in the United States.

EXAMINER: And where do your children live? Are they both with you?

CHONG: Yes, with me.

Listen to Maria

 I've had three children in my life. They were all born in Mexico.

My son Juan Carlos came to America first. He became a U.S. citizen. He helped us to come to America. He lives in Los Angeles now.

I lost my second son, Oscar, in 1998. He died in an accident. He is dead.

I don't know where my son José is. I have not seen him in 15 years. I don't know his address. He is missing.

Maria's Form

Part 11. Information About Your Children

1. Indicate your total number of children. (You must indicate **ALL** children, including: children who are alive, missing, or deceased; children born in the United States or in other countries; children under 18 years of age or older; children who are currently married or unmarried; children living with you or elsewhere; current stepchildren; legally adopted children; **and** children born when you were not married.)   `3`

2. Provide the following information about all your children (sons and daughters) listed in **Item Number 1.**, regardless of age. To list any additional children, use additional sheets of paper.

   A. Child 1

   Current Legal Name

Family Name (Last Name)	Given Name (First Name)	Middle Name (if applicable)
Perez	Juan	Carlos

A-Number (if any)	Date of Birth (mm/dd/yyyy)	Country of Birth
▶ A-	04/09/1972	Mexico

Part 11. Information About Your Children (continued)

Current Address

Street Number and Name   Apt. Ste. Flr. Number

| 1213 Roosevelt Blvd. | ☐ ☐ ☐ |

City or Town	County	State	ZIP Code + 4
Los Angeles	Los Angeles	CA	90011 - 4832

Province or Region (foreign address only)   Postal Code (foreign address only)   Country (foreign address only)

What is your child's relationship to you? (for example, biological child, stepchild, legally adopted child)   `biological child`

B. Child 2

Current Legal Name

Family Name (Last Name)	Given Name (First Name)	Middle Name (if applicable)
Perez	Oscar	n/a

A-Number (if any)

▶ A- [ ][ ][ ][ ][ ][ ][ ][ ][ ]

Date of Birth (mm/dd/yyyy) 06/17/1974

Country of Birth Mexico

Current Address

Street Number and Name N/A - deceased

Apt. ☐ Ste. ☐ Flr. ☐ Number [ ]

City or Town	County	State	ZIP Code + 4
			-

Province or Region (foreign address only)	Postal Code (foreign address only)	Country (foreign address only)

What is your child's relationship to you? (for example, biological child, stepchild, legally adopted child)

biological child

C. Child 3

Current Legal Name

Family Name (Last Name)	Given Name (First Name)	Middle Name (if applicable)
Perez	José	n/a

A-Number (if any)

▶ A- [ ][ ][ ][ ][ ][ ][ ][ ][ ]

Date of Birth (mm/dd/yyyy) 12/24/1981

Country of Birth Mexico

Part 11. Information About Your Children (continued)   A- [ ][ ][ ][ ][ ][ ][ ][ ][ ]

Current Address

Street Number and Name missing

Apt. ☐ Ste. ☐ Flr. ☐ Number [ ]

City or Town	County	State	ZIP Code + 4
			-

Province or Region (foreign address only)	Postal Code (foreign address only)	Country (foreign address only)

What is your child's relationship to you? (for example, biological child, stepchild, legally adopted child)

biological child

What Will Maria Say?

Were your children born in Mexico?

_____ a. I don't know.

_____ b. Yes.

_____ c. They are missing.

 ## Maria's Interview

EXAMINER: You have three children, is that correct?

MARIA: No. One died. Now I have only two children.

EXAMINER: Oh. I'm sorry to hear that. So you have two living children.

MARIA: Yes.

EXAMINER: And were your children born in Mexico?

MARIA: Yes.

EXAMINER: Where do they live now?

MARIA: Juan Carlos lives in Los Angeles, and I . . . José . . . I don't know where he is.

⦿ What Will You Say?

Do you have any children?
Do you have any sons or daughters?
How many children do you have?

What are their names?

What are their dates of birth?
When were they born?
What are their birth dates?

Where were they born?
In which countries were they born?

Do they live with you?
Where do they live?

Your Form

Part 11. Information About Your Children

1. Indicate your total number of children. (You must indicate **ALL** children, including: children who are alive, missing, or deceased; children born in the United States or in other countries; children under 18 years of age or older; children who are currently married or unmarried; children living with you or elsewhere; current stepchildren; legally adopted children; **and** children born when you were not married.)

2. Provide the following information about all your children (sons and daughters) listed in **Item Number 1.**, regardless of age. To list any additional children, use additional sheets of paper.

   A. Child 1

   Current Legal Name

Family Name (Last Name)	Given Name (First Name)	Middle Name (if applicable)

   A-Number (if any)   Date of Birth (mm/dd/yyyy)   Country of Birth

   ▶ A-

Part 11. Information About Your Children (continued) A- [| | | | | | | |]

Current Address

Street Number and Name   Apt. Ste. Flr. Number

[   ] ☐ ☐ ☐ [   ]

City or Town   County   State   ZIP Code + 4

[   ] [   ] [   ] [   ] - [   ]

Province or Region   Postal Code   Country
(foreign address only)   (foreign address only)   (foreign address only)

[   ] [   ] [   ]

What is your child's relationship to you? (for example, biological child,
stepchild, legally adopted child)   [   ]

B. Child 2

Current Legal Name

Family Name (Last Name)   Given Name (First Name)   Middle Name (if applicable)

[   ] [   ] [   ]

A-Number (if any)   Date of Birth (mm/dd/yyyy) Country of Birth

▶ A- [| | | | | | | |] [   ] [   ]

Current Address

Street Number and Name   Apt. Ste. Flr. Number

[   ] ☐ ☐ ☐ [   ]

City or Town   County   State   ZIP Code + 4

[   ] [   ] [   ] [   ] - [   ]

Province or Region   Postal Code   Country
(foreign address only)   (foreign address only)   (foreign address only)

[   ] [   ] [   ]

What is your child's relationship to you? (for example, biological child,
stepchild, legally adopted child)   [   ]

C. Child 3

Current Legal Name

Family Name (Last Name)   Given Name (First Name)   Middle Name (if applicable)

[   ] [   ] [   ]

A-Number (if any)   Date of Birth (mm/dd/yyyy) Country of Birth

▶ A- [| | | | | | | |] [   ] [   ]

Part 11. Information About Your Children (continued)   A- [   ]

Current Address

Street Number and Name   Apt. Ste. Flr. Number

[   ]   ☐   ☐   ☐   [   ]

City or Town   County   State   ZIP Code + 4

[   ]   [   ]   [   ]   [   ] - [   ]

Province or Region   Postal Code   Country
(foreign address only)   (foreign address only)   (foreign address only)

[   ]   [   ]   [   ]

What is your child's relationship to you? (for example, biological child,   [   ]
stepchild, legally adopted child)

D. Child 4

Current Legal Name

Family Name (Last Name)   Given Name (First Name)   Middle Name (if applicable)

[   ]   [   ]   [   ]

A-Number (if any)   Date of Birth (mm/dd/yyyy) Country of Birth

► A- [   ]   [   ]   [   ]

Current Address

Street Number and Name   Apt. Ste. Flr. Number

[   ]   ☐   ☐   ☐   [   ]

City or Town   County   State   ZIP Code + 4

[   ]   [   ]   [   ]   [   ] - [   ]

Province or Region   Postal Code   Country
(foreign address only)   (foreign address only)   (foreign address only)

[   ]   [   ]   [   ]

What is your child's relationship to you? (for example, biological child,   [   ]
stepchild, legally adopted child)

N-400 Part 12
Additional Information About You

 ## Listen to the USCIS Examiner

 Some people cannot be U.S. citizens because of things they did in the past. Here are some examples.

 ## Claiming to Be a U.S. Citizen

Ruth is a permanent resident. She is not a citizen. Six years ago, Ruth wanted a government job. The job was for U.S. citizens only. She wrote, "I am a U.S. citizen." She told the boss, "I am a U.S. citizen."

Ruth **claimed** to be a citizen. She did not tell the truth.

Maybe Ruth cannot become a citizen now. She needs to talk to a lawyer.

 ## Registering to Vote

Joseph is a permanent resident. He is not a citizen. Five years ago, Joseph **registered** to vote. He **voted** in a U.S. election.

Maybe Joseph cannot become a citizen now. He needs to talk to a lawyer.

 ## What About You?

Did you ever lie about being a U.S. citizen?

Did you ever register to vote in the U.S.?
Did you ever vote in a U.S. election?

Your Form

> **Part 12. Additional Information About You** (Person Applying for Naturalization)
>
> Answer **Item Numbers 1. - 21.** If you answer "Yes" to any of these questions, include a typed or printed explanation on additional sheets of paper.
>
> 1. Have you **EVER** claimed to be a U.S. citizen (in writing or any other way)? ☐ Yes ☐ No
>
> 2. Have you **EVER** registered to vote in any Federal, state, or local election in the United States? ☐ Yes ☐ No
>
> 3. Have you **EVER** voted in any Federal, state, or local election in the United States? ☐ Yes ☐ No

Title of Nobility

George Harris has a special **title.** He is like a king or a prince. In George's country, people do not call him Mr. Harris. They call him Sir George.

George needs to get rid of his title before he can become a citizen.

Mentally Ill

Karen is mentally ill. She does not understand what is happening around her. She is in a mental hospital.

Karen cannot become a citizen now. She is **legally incompetent.** Maybe someday she will understand what is happening. Then maybe she will become a citizen.

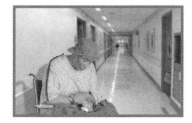

What About You?

Do people in your country call you by a special title?
Do you have a title of nobility in your native country?

Did you ever stay in a mental hospital?
Did a doctor and judge decide that you could not understand what was happening?
Did another person make decisions for you and sign papers for you?

Your Form

> 4. **A.** Do you now have, or did you **EVER** have, a hereditary title or an order of nobility in any foreign country? ☐ Yes ☐ No
>
> **B.** If you answered "Yes," are you willing to give up any inherited titles or orders of nobility that you have in a foreign country at your naturalization ceremony? ☐ Yes ☐ No
>
> 5. Have you **EVER** been declared legally incompetent or been confined to a mental institution? ☐ Yes ☐ No

◉ Failure to Pay Taxes

Jong works in a restaurant. She does not get a paycheck. Her boss pays her cash.

Jong does not pay income tax. She does not **file income tax returns.** She owes money to the government.

Before she can be a citizen, Jong needs to pay her taxes. She must pay local, state, and federal taxes for each year she worked.

◉ Claiming to Be a Nonresident

Henry is a permanent resident. But at income tax time, he does not tell the truth. He says, "I am not a U.S. resident. I am a **nonresident.** I do not need to pay taxes."

Probably Henry cannot become a U.S. citizen.

◉ What About You?

Do you work?
Do you pay state and federal income taxes every year?
Did you file income tax returns for each year you worked?
Have you paid all the taxes you owe?

Did you ever file tax returns as a nonresident?
Do you say "I am a nonresident" because you don't want to pay taxes?
Did you ever fail to pay taxes because you called yourself a nonresident?

Your Form

Part 12. Additional Information About You (Person Applying for Naturalization) (continued)	A- [ ][ ][ ][ ][ ][ ][ ][ ][ ]
6. Do you owe any overdue Federal, state, or local taxes?	☐ Yes ☐ No
7. A. Have you **EVER** not filed a Federal, state, or local tax return since you became a lawful permanent resident?	☐ Yes ☐ No
B. If you answered "Yes," did you consider yourself to be a "non-U.S. resident"?	☐ Yes ☐ No
8. Have you called yourself a "non-U.S. resident" on a Federal, state, or local tax return since you became a lawful permanent resident?	☐ Yes ☐ No

Listen to Hai

I am not a citizen yet. I have not told anyone that I am a citizen.

I have not registered to vote in U.S. elections. I never voted in a U.S. election.

I do not have a title from my country. I understand what is happening around me.

I file income taxes every year.

Hai's Form

> ### Part 12. Additional Information About You (Person Applying for Naturalization)
>
> Answer **Item Numbers 1. - 21.** If you answer "Yes" to any of these questions, include a typed or printed explanation on additional sheets of paper.
>
> 1. Have you **EVER** claimed to be a U.S. citizen (in writing or any other way)? ☐ Yes ☒ No
>
> 2. Have you **EVER** registered to vote in any Federal, state, or local election in the United States? ☐ Yes ☒ No
>
> 3. Have you **EVER** voted in any Federal, state, or local election in the United States? ☐ Yes ☒ No
>
> 4. A. Do you now have, or did you **EVER** have, a hereditary title or an order of nobility in any foreign country? ☐ Yes ☒ No
>
>   B. If you answered "Yes," are you willing to give up any inherited titles or orders of nobility that you have in a foreign country at your naturalization ceremony? ☐ Yes ☒ No
>
> 5. Have you **EVER** been declared legally incompetent or been confined to a mental institution? ☐ Yes ☒ No

> ### Part 12. Additional Information About You (Person Applying for Naturalization) (continued)
>
> 6. Do you owe any overdue Federal, state, or local taxes? ☐ Yes ☒ No
>
> 7. A. Have you **EVER** not filed a Federal, state, or local tax return since you became a lawful permanent resident? ☐ Yes ☒ No
>
>   B. If you answered "Yes," did you consider yourself to be a "non-U.S. resident"? ☐ Yes ☐ No
>
> 8. Have you called yourself a "non-U.S. resident" on a Federal, state, or local tax return since you became a lawful permanent resident? ☐ Yes ☒ No

What Will Hai Say?

Have you ever failed to file local, state, or U.S. income taxes?

_____ a. Yes.

_____ b. Federal tax returns.

_____ c. I pay my taxes every year.

Hai's Interview

EXAMINER: Have you ever claimed to be a citizen?

HAI: Claimed? You mean did I lie about it?

EXAMINER: Right.

HAI: No. I tell the truth.

EXAMINER: Have you ever registered to vote or voted in a U.S. election?

HAI: No.

EXAMINER: OK. Do you have a title of nobility from another country—a special name like a king or a prince?

HAI: No.

EXAMINER: Have you ever been declared legally incompetent?

HAI: No.

EXAMINER: What does "legally incompetent" mean?

HAI: It means your mind is not OK. Mental illness.

EXAMINER: That's right. Have you ever failed to file local, state, or U.S. income taxes?

HAI: I pay my taxes every year.

EXAMINER: Do you owe any overdue taxes?

HAI: I don't understand "overdue."

EXAMINER: Have you paid all of your taxes, or is there still some money you haven't paid yet?

HAI: No. I paid everything.

Groups You Belong To

 ## Listen to Maria

 I've been a member of the Faith Church since 2009. I also belong to the Hotel Workers' Union at my job. In Mexico, I was a member of an organization called MPDH.

Maria's Form

9. A. Have you **EVER** been a member of, involved in, or in any way associated with, any organization, association, fund, foundation, party, club, society, or similar group in the United States or in any other location in the world? ☑ Yes ☐ No

B. If you answered "Yes," provide the information below. If you need extra space, attach the names of the other groups on additional sheets of paper and provide any evidence to support your answers.

Name of the Group	Purpose of the Group	Dates of Membership	
		From (mm/dd/yyyy)	To (mm/dd/yyyy)
Faith Church	religious group	12/12/2009	present
United Hotel Workers' Union	labor organization	10/1/2005	present
Mujeres Para Derechos Humanos	promote civil rights	12/30/2001	01/14/2005

What Will Maria Say?

Are you a member of any organizations?

_____ a. Yes. Faith Church in Dallas.

_____ b. Yes, I have a job.

_____ c. I don't know any members.

Maria's Interview

EXAMINER:	Are you a member of any organizations?
MARIA:	Could you say that again?
EXAMINER:	Are you a member of any organizations?
MARIA:	I'm not sure.
EXAMINER:	For example, a club or an association?
MARIA:	Like my church?
EXAMINER:	Yes, that's an organization. So you're a member of a church?
MARIA:	Yes, Faith Church in Dallas . . . and, uh . . . let's see . . . I have a union card.
EXAMINER:	You're a union member?
MARIA:	Yes, United Hotel Workers Union, Local 21.
EXAMINER:	What about in your country?
MARIA:	In Mexico? Yes. I belonged to a group for mothers of prisoners, called Mujeres Para Derechos Humanos.

What Will You Say?

Do you belong to any groups?
Do you belong to a church or a union?
Do you belong to a club or an organization?
Have you ever belonged to any groups in the U.S.?

Were you a member of any groups in your country?

Your Form

9. **A.** Have you **EVER** been a member of, involved in, or in any way associated with, any organization, association, fund, foundation, party, club, society, or similar group in the United States or in any other location in the world?　☐ Yes ☐ No

   B. If you answered "Yes," provide the information below. If you need extra space, attach the names of the other groups on additional sheets of paper and provide any evidence to support your answers.

Name of the Group	Purpose of the Group	Dates of Membership	
		From (mm/dd/yyyy)	To (mm/dd/yyyy)

Listen to the USCIS Examiner

 Some people belong to groups that do not agree with the United States. Some people belong to groups that the U.S. does not agree with. Some people belong to groups that want to hurt the United States. Some people think that it's OK to hurt other people.

A person who does these things cannot become a U.S. citizen. Here are some examples.

 ## Communist

Li Xian is still a member of the **Communist Party** in her country. She believes in Communism.

Li Xian cannot be a citizen.

 ## Totalitarian Party

Many years ago in Spain, Juan was a leader in a **totalitarian** group. This group hurt and killed people who did not agree with them. They put many people in jail for trying to stop them.

Probably Juan cannot be a citizen.

 ## Terrorist Organization

Chuck belongs to a group that does not like the United States. His group put a bomb in a building. The bomb killed many people.

Chuck is a member of a **terrorist** organization. This group wants a different government. They plan to fight a war with the United States. They want to fight with guns and bombs. They want to overthrow the U.S. government by force.

Chuck cannot become a U.S. citizen.

Listen to Sergei

 I was a doctor in the Soviet Union. I did not want to join the Communist Party. But only party members could work in my hospital. For doctors, joining the Communist Party was **compulsory.** I am not a member of the Communist Party any more.

I was a soldier in the Soviet Army, too. It was compulsory for all men in my country. If you served in the military for your country, you must write it on your form. And if you check the "yes" box for any of the questions in Part 12, you have to write a note to explain your answer.

Sergei's Form

9. **A.** Have you **EVER** been a member of, involved in, or in any way associated with, any organization, association, fund, foundation, party, club, society, or similar group in the United States or in any other location in the world?   ☒ Yes ☐ No

    B. If you answered "Yes," provide the information below. If you need extra space, attach the names of the other groups on additional sheets of paper and provide any evidence to support your answers.

Name of the Group	Purpose of the Group	Dates of Membership	
		From (mm/dd/yyyy)	To (mm/dd/yyyy)
Soviet Communist Party	political	09/12/1969	03/25/1990

10. Have you **EVER** been a member of, or in any way associated (either directly or indirectly) with:

    A. The Communist Party?   ☒ Yes ☐ No

    B. Any other totalitarian party?   ☐ Yes ☒ No

    C. A terrorist organization?   ☐ Yes ☒ No

Dear USCIS,

I was a member of the Communist Party from 1969 to 1990 because it was required for my job. It was compulsory. In 1990 I ended my membership in the Communist Party.

          Thank you,

          Sergei Petrov

What Will Sergei Say?

When was that?

_____ a. From 1969 to 1990.

_____ b. Russia.

_____ c. 21 years.

Sergei's Interview

EXAMINER: Have you ever been a member of any organizations?

SERGEI: In the U.S. or in my old country?

EXAMINER: Both.

SERGEI: I was a Communist Party member for my job in the Soviet Union. It was compulsory.

EXAMINER: When was that?

SERGEI: From 1969 to 1990. I have an affidavit—a letter—to explain this.

What About You?

Have you ever been a member of the Communist Party?

Have you ever been a member of a totalitarian party?

Are you a member of a terrorist organization?
Have you ever been a member of a terrorist organization?

Your Form

10.	Have you **EVER** been a member of, or in any way associated (either directly or indirectly) with:		
	A. The Communist Party?	☐ Yes	☐ No
	B. Any other totalitarian party?	☐ Yes	☐ No
	C. A terrorist organization?	☐ Yes	☐ No

Overthrow Government

Sulim lived in a part of Russia. But he did not like the Russian Government. He joined a group that fought Russia with guns and bombs. His group was violent. They used force to try to overthrow their country's government.

Sulim cannot become a citizen.

Persecuted People

Herman belonged to a group of white men in South Africa. His group did not like black people. He hurt people who were different from him. Herman **persecuted** people.

Probably Herman cannot become a U.S. citizen.

What About You?

Do you want to fight a war against the government of the United States?
Have you ever told people that they should fight a war against the U.S. government?

Have you ever told people that they should fight a war against another country?

Have you ever advocated for the overthrow of a government?
Did you use force or violence?

Did you ever hurt anyone because
• they looked different from you?
• they belonged to a different religion?
• they came from a different place?
• you did not agree with the things they believed?

Your Form

11.	Have you **EVER** advocated (either directly or indirectly) the overthrow of any government by force or violence?	☐ Yes ☐ No
12.	Have you **EVER** persecuted (either directly or indirectly) any person because of race, religion, national origin, membership in a particular social group, or political opinion?	☐ Yes ☐ No

Nazi Government

Hans was a **Nazi** in Germany during World War II.

Hans cannot become a U.S. citizen.

 ## What About You?

Did you work for the Nazi government of Germany between 1933 and 1945?
Did you help the Nazi government in World War II?

Your Form

13.	Between March 23, 1933 and May 8, 1945, did you work for or associate in any way (either directly or indirectly) with:

A. The Nazi government of Germany? ☐ Yes ☐ No

B. Any government in any area occupied by, allied with, or established with the help of the Nazi government of Germany? ☐ Yes ☐ No

C. Any German, Nazi, or S.S. military unit, paramilitary unit, self-defense unit, vigilante unit, citizen unit, police unit, government agency or office, extermination camp, concentration camp, prisoner of war camp, prison, labor camp, or transit camp? ☐ Yes ☐ No

Human Rights and War Crimes

Listen to the USCIS Examiner

All people have the right to be treated with respect. All people have human rights. Sometimes we do not agree with other people. But it is not OK to hurt or kill someone just because you do not agree with them. Even criminals and prisoners of war have rights.

Genocide

Eng was a leader in a group did not respect human rights. Eng's group killed thousands of people in Cambodia. They committed **genocide.**

Torture

When people did something that Eng did not like, he **hurt** them very badly. Eng **tortured** many people.

Forced Sexual Relations

Bernard was the leader of a group of fighters in Rwanda. His group **forced** women and girls to do something they did not want to do. He forced them to have **sexual relations** with the soldiers.

Bernard cannot become a citizen.

Not Letting People Practice Their Religion

Eng killed people who tried to practice their religion.

Eng cannot become a citizen.

 ## What About You?

Have you ever killed or tortured anyone?
Have you ever tried to kill anyone?
Have you ever forced someone to have sexual relations?
Have you ever stopped another person from practicing his or her religion?

Your Form

Part 12. Additional Information About You (Person Applying for Naturalization) (continued)	A-

14. Were you **EVER** involved in any way with any of the following:

    A. Genocide? ☐ Yes ☐ No

    B. Torture? ☐ Yes ☐ No

    C. Killing, or trying to kill, someone? ☐ Yes ☐ No

    D. Badly hurting, or trying to hurt, a person on purpose? ☐ Yes ☐ No

    E. Forcing, or trying to force, someone to have any kind of sexual contact or relations? ☐ Yes ☐ No

    F. Not letting someone practice his or her religion? ☐ Yes ☐ No

Military Groups

Listen to the USCIS Examiner

 There are many kinds of military groups. For example, Sergei was a soldier in the Russian Army. The Russian Army is a **military unit.** It uses **weapons** like guns and bombs and tanks. But Sergei followed his country's laws. He respected human rights.

Sergei can become a citizen.

Eng was also in a **military unit.** His group fought against the government of his country with many kinds of weapons. It did not follow the laws. It did not respect human rights. There are different names for a group like this. It may be called a **rebel group,** a **guerilla group,** or an **insurgent group.**

Eng cannot become a U.S. citizen.

Tomas was a soldier in a **paramilitary** group in El Salvador. He was part of a **militia.** This group looked like an army, and they acted like an army. Sometimes they helped the army. But they were not part of the real Salvadoran Army, and they did not follow the laws. They did not respect human rights.

Tomas cannot become a citizen.

◉ Listen to the USCIS Examiner

There are different kinds of police groups, too. For example, Otto was a member of a police unit in Germany. He carried a gun. But he followed the laws of his country. He respected human rights.

Otto can become a citizen.

Kevin was a member of a **vigilante** group in Ireland. His group acted like the police, but they were not the police. They used guns and sometimes they killed people. They did not follow the laws. They did not respect human rights.

Kevin cannot become a citizen.

◉ What Will You Say?

Have you ever been a member of a military group?
Were you a member of a military or paramilitary unit in your country?
Have you ever been a member in a police unit?
Were you part of a vigilante or self-defense unit in your country?
Have you ever been part of a rebel group or a guerilla group?
Have you ever been part of a militia or insurgent organization?

Your Form

15.	Were you **EVER** a member of, or did you **EVER** serve in, help, or otherwise participate in, any of the following groups:		
A.	Military unit?	☐ Yes	☐ No
B.	Paramilitary unit (a group of people who act like a military group but are not part of the official military)?	☐ Yes	☐ No
C.	Police unit?	☐ Yes	☐ No
D.	Self-defense unit?	☐ Yes	☐ No
E.	Vigilante unit (a group of people who act like the police, but are not part of the official police)?	☐ Yes	☐ No
F.	Rebel group?	☐ Yes	☐ No
G.	Guerrilla group (a group of people who use weapons against or otherwise physically attack the military, police, government, or other people)?	☐ Yes	☐ No
H.	Militia (an army of people, not part of the official military)?	☐ Yes	☐ No
I.	Insurgent organization (a group that uses weapons and fights against a government)?	☐ Yes	☐ No

Prison, Detention, and Labor Camps

Carlos was the leader of a **detention center** in Chile. He took people from their homes and he put them in a secret prison. He forced them to tell their secrets. He tortured them to get information. He did not respect human rights. Carlos cannot become a citizen.

Sung-ho was the leader of a **labor camp** in North Korea. He forced prisoners to work all day, every day for no pay. Many of them worked until they died. Sung-ho cannot become a citizen.

Juan worked in a **prison,** too. The prisoners were in jail because a judge decided that they had broken the law. Juan did not hurt the prisoners. He respected their human rights. Juan can become a citizen.

What Will You Say?

Have you ever worked in a prison or detention facility?
Have you ever worked in a labor camp?
Have you ever worked in a place where people were forced to stay?

Your Form

16.	Were you **EVER** a worker, volunteer, or soldier, or did you otherwise **EVER** serve in any of the following:		
	A. Prison or jail?	☐ Yes	☐ No
	B. Prison camp?	☐ Yes	☐ No
	C. Detention facility (a place where people are forced to stay)?	☐ Yes	☐ No
	D. Labor camp (a place where people are forced to work)?	☐ Yes	☐ No
	E. Any other place where people were forced to stay?	☐ Yes	☐ No

Weapons

Listen to the USCIS Examiner

When people use or **sell weapons,** they do not always respect human rights. They sometimes use weapons to commit war crimes.

For example, Tomas used guns to kill men, women, and children in his country. He **sold weapons** to make money for his paramilitary group. He **gave weapons** to other paramilitary groups.

Tomas trained other fighters to use guns and bombs. He gave them **military training.** He knew that these fighters would kill men, women, and children in El Salvador. Tomas cannot become a citizen.

Police officers and soldiers often use weapons. But that does not mean they are committing war crimes. For example, when Juan was a prison guard, he learned to use a gun. The prison gave him **weapons training.** He sometimes said to a prisoner, "Stop, or I will shoot you." If the prisoner did not stop, Juan fired his gun. He shot at the prisoner.

Juan did not sell weapons to anybody. He did not give weapons to anybody.

He did not commit war crimes.

Juan has to check the "yes" boxes in questions 17 and 19. He needs to write a note to explain his answers. But he can still become a citizen.

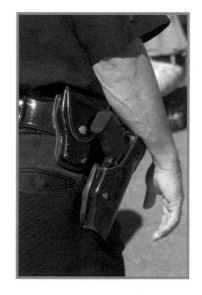

Dear USCIS,
I was a guard in Alta prison in Lima, Peru from 1990 to 1998.
I used a gun. I had to shoot at prisoners if they tried to escape.
The prison gave me weapons training. It was part of my job.

Juan Ramirez

Juan's Form

17. Were you **EVER** a part of any group, or did you **EVER** help any group, unit, or organization that used a weapon against any person, or threatened to do so? ☒ Yes ☐ No

    A. If you answered "Yes," when you were part of this group, or when you helped this group, did you ever use a weapon against another person? ☒ Yes ☐ No

    B. If you answered "Yes," when you were part of this group, or when you helped this group, did you ever tell another person that you would use a weapon against that person? ☒ Yes ☐ No

18. Did you **EVER** sell, give, or provide weapons to any person, or help another person sell, give, or provide weapons to any person? ☐ Yes ☒ No

    A. If you answered "Yes," did you know that this person was going to use the weapons against another person? ☐ Yes ☐ No

    B. If you answered "Yes," did you know that this person was going to sell or give the weapons to someone who was going to use them against another person? ☐ Yes ☐ No

19. Did you **EVER** receive any type of military, paramilitary (a group of people who act like a military group but are not part of the official military), or weapons training? ☒ Yes ☐ No

◉ What Will You Say?

Did you ever use a weapon against another person?

Were you ever a member of a group that fought with weapons?

Did you ever tell anyone that you would use a weapon against them?

Did you ever shoot a gun at anyone?

Did you ever sell weapons to anyone? Or give weapons to anyone?

Have you ever had any kind of military or paramilitary training?

Have you ever received training in how to use weapons?

Your Form

17. Were you **EVER** a part of any group, or did you **EVER** help any group, unit, or organization that used a weapon against any person, or threatened to do so? ☐ Yes ☐ No

    A. If you answered "Yes," when you were part of this group, or when you helped this group, did you ever use a weapon against another person? ☐ Yes ☐ No

    B. If you answered "Yes," when you were part of this group, or when you helped this group, did you ever tell another person that you would use a weapon against that person? ☐ Yes ☐ No

18. Did you **EVER** sell, give, or provide weapons to any person, or help another person sell, give, or provide weapons to any person? ☐ Yes ☐ No

    A. If you answered "Yes," did you know that this person was going to use the weapons against another person? ☐ Yes ☐ No

    B. If you answered "Yes," did you know that this person was going to sell or give the weapons to someone who was going to use them against another person? ☐ Yes ☐ No

19. Did you **EVER** receive any type of military, paramilitary (a group of people who act like a military group but are not part of the official military), or weapons training? ☐ Yes ☐ No

Conscripting Child Soldiers

Joseph was the leader of a rebel group in Africa. He needed more soldiers so he got children to work in his army. Sometimes the children wanted to work for him. Most of the time he took the children from their homes. He **forced** them to be **child soldiers.** He forced them to work in his army.

 ## What Will You Say?

Did you ever ask a child, or force a child to be a soldier?
Did you ever put a child to work helping soldiers to fight a war?

Your Form

20.	Did you **EVER** recruit (ask), enlist (sign up), conscript (require), or use any person under 15 years of age to serve in or help an armed force or group?	☐ Yes	☐ No
21.	Did you **EVER** use any person under 15 years of age to do anything that helped or supported people in combat?	☐ Yes	☐ No

Arrests and Crimes

 ## Listen to the USCIS Examiner

 If you have had any problem with the police, you must tell USCIS. If you have been to court for any problems, you must tell USCIS. If you have had any problems with the law, it is a good idea to talk to a lawyer before you apply for citizenship—

- even if it happened a long time ago
- even if it was not your fault
- even if you think it is not on your record
- even if it happened when you were a child

After taking your fingerprints, USCIS will find out about any problems. Even old problems. Even small problems.

Be careful when you answer these questions.

At your interview, you must tell the truth about what happened.

Listen to Ahmed

 Thirty years ago the police **arrested** me. I was arrested because of a fight. The police said that I hit a man. I was charged with assault. Assault is a **crime.** It's against the law.

The judge did not send me to jail. She put me on parole.

After that, for 30 years, I never had problems with police. When I filled out my application, I did not think a problem from a long time ago was important. Question 16 asks, "Have you ever been arrested?" I checked No on question 16.

I did not tell the truth.

Ahmed's Interview

EXAMINER: Have you ever committed a crime?

AHMED: No.

EXAMINER: Are you sure? You've never been arrested?

AHMED: No.

EXAMINER: I have a report from the FBI. It says that you were arrested in New York for assault in 1982. Do you know anything about that?

AHMED: Well, yes. I was arrested, but it was a mistake.

EXAMINER: On your application, you wrote that you have never been arrested. Is that true or a mistake?

AHMED: I don't know. I was arrested, but I never went to jail. That's why I didn't write anything on my application about it.

EXAMINER: I know it was a long time ago, and maybe it was not very serious. But you did not tell the truth. This is a very serious problem for your application.

Listen to Maria

Four years ago, a police officer stopped my car. He said that my car needed a new inspection sticker. I had to pay a fine and get a new inspection sticker. I have not had any other problems with the police.

Maria's Form

If any of Item Numbers 22. - 28. apply to you, you must answer "Yes" even if your records have been sealed, expunged, or otherwise cleared. You must disclose this information even if someone, including a judge, law enforcement officer, or attorney, told you that it no longer constitutes a record or told you that you do not have to disclose the information.

22. Have you **EVER** committed, assisted in committing, or attempted to commit, a crime or offense for which you were **NOT** arrested? ☐ Yes ☑ No

23. Have you **EVER** been arrested, cited, or detained by any law enforcement officer (including any immigration official or any official of the U.S. armed forces) for any reason? ☑ Yes ☐ No

24. Have you **EVER** been charged with committing, attempting to commit, or assisting in committing a crime or offense? ☐ Yes ☑ No

25. Have you **EVER** been convicted of a crime or offense? ☐ Yes ☑ No

26. Have you **EVER** been placed in an alternative sentencing or a rehabilitative program (for example, diversion, deferred prosecution, withheld adjudication, deferred adjudication)? ☐ Yes ☑ No

27. A. Have you **EVER** received a suspended sentence, been placed on probation, or been paroled? ☐ Yes ☑ No

   B. If you answered "Yes," have you completed the probation or parole? ☐ Yes ☐ No

28. A. Have you **EVER** been in jail or prison? ☐ Yes ☑ No

   B. If you answered "Yes," how long were you in jail or prison? Years [ ] Months [ ] Days [ ]

29. If you answered "No" to **ALL** questions in **Item Numbers 23. - 28.**, then skip this item and go to **Item Number 30.**

   If you answered "Yes" to any question in **Item Numbers 23. - 28.**, then complete this table. If you need extra space, use additional sheets of paper and provide any evidence to support your answers.

Why were you arrested, cited, detained, or charged?	Date arrested, cited, detained, or charged. (mm/dd/yyyy)	Where were you arrested, cited, detained, or charged? (City or Town, State, Country)	Outcome or disposition of the arrest, citation, detention, or charge (no charges filed, charges dismissed, jail, probation, etc.)
expired car inspection sticker	02/09/2008	Dallas, TX, USA	no charges filed

What Will Maria Say?

Have you ever been in jail?

_____ a. I paid a fine.

_____ b. Prison.

_____ c. No.

 ## Maria's Interview

EXAMINER: Have you ever committed a crime?

MARIA: Crime?

EXAMINER: Have you ever done anything illegal—anything that was against the law?

MARIA: No.

EXAMINER: Have you ever been arrested, cited, or detained by the police?

MARIA: What is "detained"?

EXAMINER: Have you ever been in jail?

MARIA: No. But once I had to pay a fine because of my inspection sticker.

EXAMINER: Have you ever been to court? Did a judge say that something you did was not OK?

MARIA: No.

 ## What Will You Say?

Did you ever break the law?

Have you ever committed a crime?

Have you ever been arrested?

Have you ever had a problem with the police?

Have you ever been to court?

Have you ever been charged or convicted of a crime?

Have you ever been on parole?

Have you ever been in jail?

Your Form

If any of Item Numbers 22. - 28. apply to you, you must answer "Yes" even if your records have been sealed, expunged, or otherwise cleared. You must disclose this information even if someone, including a judge, law enforcement officer, or attorney, told you that it no longer constitutes a record or told you that you do not have to disclose the information.

22. Have you **EVER** committed, assisted in committing, or attempted to commit, a crime or offense for which you were **NOT** arrested? ☐ Yes ☐ No

23. Have you **EVER** been arrested, cited, or detained by any law enforcement officer (including any immigration official or any official of the U.S. armed forces) for any reason? ☐ Yes ☐ No

24. Have you **EVER** been charged with committing, attempting to commit, or assisting in committing a crime or offense? ☐ Yes ☐ No

25. Have you **EVER** been convicted of a crime or offense? ☐ Yes ☐ No

26. Have you **EVER** been placed in an alternative sentencing or a rehabilitative program (for example, diversion, deferred prosecution, withheld adjudication, deferred adjudication)? ☐ Yes ☐ No

27. A. Have you **EVER** received a suspended sentence, been placed on probation, or been paroled? ☐ Yes ☐ No

    B. If you answered "Yes," have you completed the probation or parole? ☐ Yes ☐ No

28. A. Have you **EVER** been in jail or prison? ☐ Yes ☐ No

    B. If you answered "Yes," how long were you in jail or prison? Years ☐ Months ☐ Days ☐

29. If you answered "No" to **ALL** questions in **Item Numbers 23. - 28.**, then skip this item and go to **Item Number 30.**

    If you answered "Yes" to any question in **Item Numbers 23. - 28.**, then complete this table. If you need extra space, use additional sheets of paper and provide any evidence to support your answers.

Why were you arrested, cited, detained, or charged?	Date arrested, cited, detained, or charged. (mm/dd/yyyy)	Where were you arrested, cited, detained, or charged? (City or Town, State, Country)	Outcome or disposition of the arrest, citation, detention, or charge (no charges filed, charges dismissed, jail, probation, etc.)

Habitual Drunkard

Albert drinks a lot of alcohol. He is **drunk** every day.

Probably Albert cannot become a citizen.

Prostitute

Estela is a **prostitute.**
Men pay her money to sleep with them.

Probably Estela cannot become a citizen.
The men who have sex with Estela probably cannot become citizens either.

Controlled Substances

Tu sells **illegal drugs** like marijuana, cocaine, and heroin.

Tu cannot become a citizen.

What About You?

Do you get drunk every day?
Do you drink too much alcohol?
Have you ever had problems with drinking?

Did you ever get paid for having sex?
Did you ever pay someone to sleep with you?
Did you ever buy or sell sex?

Do you sell drugs?
Did you ever sell drugs?
Have you ever had any problems with marijuana or cocaine?
Did you ever bring illegal drugs into this country?

Your Form

Answer **Item Numbers 30. - 46.** If you answer "Yes" to any of these questions, except **Item Numbers 37.** and **38.**, include a typed or printed explanation on additional sheets of paper and provide any evidence to support your answers.

30. Have you **EVER**:

    A. Been a habitual drunkard? ☐ Yes ☐ No

    B. Been a prostitute, or procured anyone for prostitution? ☐ Yes ☐ No

    C. Sold or smuggled controlled substances, illegal drugs, or narcotics? ☐ Yes ☐ No

Married to More Than One Person

Chimme has two wives. This is OK in his country. It's not OK in the U.S.

He cannot become a citizen.

 ## Marriage Fraud

Lara wanted to get a green card. She paid a U.S. citizen $10,000 to marry her. It was not a real marriage. They did not live together or share their money together.

Lara cannot become a citizen.

 ## Helped Anyone Enter the U.S. Illegally

Manuel helps people come to the U.S. These people do not have green cards. They do not have visas. They pay Manuel a lot of money. He helps them **enter the U.S. illegally.**

Manuel cannot become a citizen.

 ## What About You?

Have you ever been married to two people at the same time?

Did you get married so you could get a green card?
Did you lie about your marriage on your immigration papers?

Did you ever help someone come to the U.S. without a visa?
Did you ever help anyone enter the U.S. illegally?

Your Form

		Yes	No
D.	Been married to more than one person at the same time?	☐ Yes	☐ No
E.	Married someone in order to obtain an immigration benefit?	☐ Yes	☐ No
F.	Helped anyone to enter, or try to enter, the United States illegally?	☐ Yes	☐ No

Gambled Illegally

Sin likes to play cards. He wants to win a lot of money. He does not play in a casino. He plays in secret. He plays where the police cannot see him. Sin likes **gambling.**

Probably Sin cannot become a citizen.

Failed to Support Dependents

Raul left his wife and children. He does not send them any money. He does not support his dependents. He does not pay his wife any money. He has failed to pay **alimony** or **child support.**

Probably Raul cannot become a citizen.

Lied to Get Benefits

Luc wanted to get food stamps and live in public housing. He said he was a U.S. citizen on the application forms. Luc lied so he could get benefits.

Luc cannot become a citizen.

What About You?

Do you play cards for money?
Do you play in secret?
Did you ever take money from illegal gambling?

Do your children live with you?
Do you support your children?
Are you required to make child support payments?
Have you ever failed to pay alimony?
Have you ever failed to support your family?

Do you receive any public benefits, like food stamps, SSI, or public housing?
Did you lie on your application forms so you could get these benefits?

Your Form

G.	Gambled illegally or received income from illegal gambling?	☐ Yes	☐ No
H.	Failed to support your dependents or to pay alimony?	☐ Yes	☐ No
I.	Made any misrepresentation to obtain any public benefit in the United States?	☐ Yes	☐ No

False or Misleading Information

Boris wanted to come to America. But he didn't get a visa. He found a woman with a green card. He paid the woman to say that she was his mother. He used papers that were not real. He came to America and got a green card.

He did not tell the truth. He **lied** to USCIS. He lied to the government.

Boris cannot be a citizen.

What About You?

Did you ever tell the government something that was not true?
Did you write anything on your USCIS forms that was not true?
Did you lie to get your green card? Did you lie to get a visa?
Did you lie to the government so that you could stay in the U.S.?

Your Form

31.	Have you **EVER** given any U.S. Government officials **any** information or documentation that was false, fraudulent, or misleading?	☐ Yes ☐ No
32.	Have you **EVER** lied to any U.S. Government officials to gain entry or admission into the United States or to gain immigration benefits while in the United States?	☐ Yes ☐ No

Removal and Deportation

Ordered Deported

Ten years ago, Julio was **deported.** A judge said, "You must go back to your country. You cannot stay in the United States."

Probably Julio cannot become a citizen. He should talk to a lawyer.

What About You?

Did USCIS ever tell you that you must go back to your country?
Did a judge order you to leave the U.S.?

Your Form

33.	Have you **EVER** been removed, excluded, or deported from the United States?	☐ Yes ☐ No
34.	Have you **EVER** been ordered removed, excluded, or deported from the United States?	☐ Yes ☐ No
35.	Have you **EVER** been placed in removal, exclusion, rescission, or deportation proceedings?	☐ Yes ☐ No
36.	Are removal, exclusion, rescission, or deportation proceedings (including administratively closed proceedings) **currently** pending against you?	☐ Yes ☐ No

Military Service

 ## Deserted from U.S. Armed Forces

When Paul was young, he was a soldier in the U.S. Army. He served in the Armed Forces.

Paul did not like being in the army. He ran away. He **deserted** from the U.S. Armed Forces.

Maybe Paul cannot be a citizen. He needs to talk to a lawyer.

 ## What About You?

Have you ever served in the U.S. Armed Forces?

Are you a member of the U.S. Armed Forces?

Have you ever left the U.S. so that you would not have to serve in the Armed Forces?

Have you ever told the government that you could not serve in the Armed Forces?

If you were a soldier, did you ever desert from the Armed Forces?

Your Form

37.	Have you **EVER** served in the U.S. armed forces?	☐ Yes ☐ No
38. A.	Are you **currently** a member of the U.S. armed forces?	☐ Yes ☐ No
B.	If you answered "Yes," are you scheduled to deploy overseas, including to a vessel, within the next three months? (Refer to the **Address Change** section in the Instructions on how to notify USCIS if you learn of your deployment plans after you file your Form N-400.)	☐ Yes ☐ No
C.	If you answered "Yes," are you **currently** stationed overseas?	☐ Yes ☐ No
39.	Have you **EVER** been court-martialed, administratively separated, or disciplined, or have you received an other than honorable discharge, while in the U.S. armed forces?	☐ Yes ☐ No
40.	Have you **EVER** been discharged from training or service in the U.S. armed forces because you were an alien?	☐ Yes ☐ No
41.	Have you **EVER** left the United States to avoid being drafted in the U.S. armed forces?	☐ Yes ☐ No
42.	Have you **EVER** applied for any kind of exemption from military service in the U.S. armed forces?	☐ Yes ☐ No
43.	Have you **EVER** deserted from the U.S. armed forces?	☐ Yes ☐ No

Selective Service Registration

Did Not Register with Selective Service System

In America, all men must register for **Selective Service** when they are 18 years old. Every man must be registered until he is 26 years old. Most men register at the Post Office.

Hai came to the U.S. when he was 24. He did not know about the Selective Service law. He did not register. The N-400 application says that men who are younger than 26 must be registered before they apply for citizenship. Men who are older than 31 do not need to worry about this problem. Hai is older than 31.

But if you are a man between the ages of 26 and 31, and you did not register for Selective Service, you must explain this to USCIS. You need to tell why you did not register. And you need to get a status information letter from Selective Service to send with your application.

Men who are now:

18–25   register now

26–31   explain why you didn't register and get a status information letter

32 or older   no action needed

◉ What About You?

If you are a man:

- Are you between the ages of 18 and 26?
- Were you a resident of the U.S. when you were between the ages of 18 and 26?
- (If you answered Yes) Did you register for Selective Service?

Your Form

Part 12. Additional Information About You (Person Applying for Naturalization) (continued)

A- [ ][ ][ ][ ][ ][ ][ ][ ][ ]

44. **A.** Are you a male who lived in the United States at any time between your 18th and 26th birthdays? (This does not include living in the United States as a lawful nonimmigrant.) ☐ Yes ☐ No

B. If you answered "Yes," when did you register for the Selective Service? Provide the information below.

Date Registered (mm/dd/yyyy)

Selective Service Number

[ ][ ][ ][ ][ ][ ][ ][ ][ ][ ]

C. If you answered "Yes," but you **did not register** with the Selective Service System and you are:

1. Still under 26 years of age, you must register before you apply for naturalization, and complete the Selective Service information above; **OR**

2. Now 26 to 31 years of age (29 years of age if you are filing under INA section 319(a)), but you did not register with the Selective Service, you must attach a statement explaining why you did not register, and provide a status information letter from the Selective Service.

Oath Requirements

◉ Listen to Maria

I believe in the government of the United States. I agree with the form of government America has. I believe in the Constitution. I agree with the laws of this country.

I am ready to take the Oath of Allegiance to the United States.

What Will Maria Say?

Do you support the Constitution and form of government of the United States?

_____ a. I love my country.

_____ b. No, I don't.

_____ c. Yes, I do.

◉ What About You?

Do you agree with the form of government of the United States?
Do you agree with the Constitution of the United States?
Do you support the Constitution and form of government of the U.S.?

Your Form

45. Do you support the Constitution and form of Government of the United States?	☐ Yes ☐ No

Listen to the USCIS Examiner

The Oath of Allegiance is a promise that you make when you become a citizen. The words are old and difficult to understand—even for people who speak English very well.

Listen to the oath. I will explain each part.

oath: **I hereby declare, on oath . . .**

meaning: I promise today.

oath: **. . . that I absolutely and entirely renounce and abjure all allegiance and fidelity to any foreign prince, potentate, state, or sovereignty, of whom or which I have heretofore been a subject or citizen . . .**

meaning: I am not a citizen of my old country anymore. I am a citizen of the U.S. now.

oath: **. . . that I will support and defend the Constitution and laws of the United States of America . . .**

meaning: I believe in the Constitution and the laws of the United States, and I will support them.

oath: **. . . against all enemies, foreign and domestic . . .**

meaning: I will not let anyone—from this country or from any other country—take away our form of government.

oath: **. . . that I will bear true faith and allegiance to the same . . .**

meaning: I will be loyal to my country and to the Constitution.

oath: **. . . that I will bear arms on behalf of the United States when required by the law . . .**

meaning: If my country needs me, I will fight in the Armed Forces.

oath: **. . . that I will perform noncombatant service in the Armed Forces of the United States when required by the law . . .**

meaning: If my country needs me, I will do work to help the Armed Forces.

oath: **. . . that I will perform work of national importance under civilian direction when required by the law . . .**

meaning: If my country needs me, I will do work in my community.

oath: **. . . and that I take this obligation freely, without any mental reservation or purpose of evasion . . .**

meaning: I agree that this is my choice and that no one is forcing me or scaring me into making this promise.

oath: **. . . so help me God.**

meaning: Let God hear my words.

◉ Listen to Hai

The United States is my country now. I promise to love my country in good times and in bad times too.

I hope we will always have peace in the United States. But if there is a war someday, I must be ready to help. If the government asks me to fight, I will say yes.

Maybe someday there will be an emergency. If the government asks me to help, I will say yes.

What Will Hai Say?

Do you support the Constitution and form of government of the United States?

_____ a. Yes, I do.

_____ b. No, I don't.

_____ c. It is the highest law.

◉ Hai's Interview

EXAMINER: Do you support the Constitution and form of government of the United States?

HAI: Yes, I do.

EXAMINER: This is the Oath of Allegiance. Please read it and tell me if you are willing to take this oath. Do you understand what the oath means? Can you tell me in your own words?

HAI: I understand. It means that I promise to love my country in good times and in bad times.

EXAMINER: Are you willing to bear arms for your country?

HAI: Bear arms? You mean carry a gun?

EXAMINER: Yes. If the United States needed you, would you fight in the Armed Forces?

HAI: This is my country now. I stand with my country always. In peace and in war.

Listen to Maria

I am an old woman. I know the U.S. will never want me to be a soldier in the army. But I will promise to help my country anyway.

I will promise to help in a war or emergency if my country needs me.

Maria's Form

Answer **Item Numbers 45. - 50.** If you answer "No" to any of these questions, include a typed or printed explanation on additional sheets of paper and provide any evidence to support your answers.

45. Do you support the Constitution and form of Government of the United States? ☑ Yes ☐ No

46. Do you understand the full Oath of Allegiance to the United States? ☑ Yes ☐ No

47. Are you willing to take the full Oath of Allegiance to the United States? ☑ Yes ☐ No

48. If the law requires it, are you willing to bear arms on behalf of the United States? ☑ Yes ☐ No

49. If the law requires it, are you willing to perform noncombatant services in the U.S. armed forces? ☑ Yes ☐ No

50. If the law requires it, are you willing to perform work of national importance under civilian direction? ☑ Yes ☐ No

What Will Maria Say?

If there was a war, would you fight for the U.S.?

_____ a. I am an old woman!

_____ b. Yes.

_____ c. My new country.

Maria's Interview

EXAMINER: If the law requires it, are you willing to bear arms on behalf of the U.S.?

MARIA: I don't know what "bear arms" means.

EXAMINER: If there was a war, would you fight for the U.S.?

MARIA: Yes.

EXAMINER: Even against your old country? What if the U.S. fought a war against Mexico?

MARIA: A war against Mexico?

EXAMINER: Yes. Would you fight for the U.S. even if that happened?

MARIA: Yes. If I am a U.S. citizen, I have to fight for the United States.

Religious Exemptions

Listen to Susan

I want to be a U.S. citizen. But I cannot promise to fight in a war.

My church teaches me that I can follow only God. I cannot promise to follow any government. I cannot take an oath.

Two elders from my church helped me write a letter to USCIS. The letter explained why I cannot make these promises. They also wrote a letter to show that I have been a member of my church for a long time.

Susan's Form

Answer **Item Numbers 45. - 50.** If you answer "No" to any of these questions, include a typed or printed explanation on additional sheets of paper and provide any evidence to support your answers.

45.	Do you support the Constitution and form of Government of the United States?	☒ Yes ☐ No
46.	Do you understand the full Oath of Allegiance to the United States?	☒ Yes ☐ No
47.	Are you willing to take the full Oath of Allegiance to the United States?	☐ Yes ☒ No
48.	If the law requires it, are you willing to bear arms on behalf of the United States?	☐ Yes ☒ No
49.	If the law requires it, are you willing to perform noncombatant services in the U.S. armed forces?	☐ Yes ☒ No
50.	If the law requires it, are you willing to perform work of national importance under civilian direction?	☒ Yes ☐ No

What Will Susan Say?

How long have you been a member of this church?

_____ a. Jehovah's Witness.

_____ b. Since 2009.

_____ c. I answer to God.

Susan's Interview

EXAMINER: Are you willing to take the Oath of Allegiance to the U.S.?

SUSAN: No. My church teaches me that I cannot take any oath.

EXAMINER: Why is that?

SUSAN: Because I can answer only to God. I cannot answer to any person or government.

EXAMINER: Are you willing to bear arms on behalf of the U.S.? I mean, would you fight in a war if the government asked you to?

SUSAN: No. My church teaches me that I cannot fight in any war.

EXAMINER: What about noncombatant services in the Armed Forces?

SUSAN: You mean work for the army?

EXAMINER: Yes. Can you serve in the Armed Forces as a nurse or a mechanic?

SUSAN: No. My church teaches that we cannot work for the army because we would be helping the soldiers to kill other people.

EXAMINER: Can you perform work of national importance under civilian direction?

SUSAN: I don't understand.

EXAMINER: Are you willing to help in your community in a time of emergency—for example, a flood or an earthquake?

SUSAN: Yes. If it's outside of the army, I can do that.

EXAMINER: What is your church?

SUSAN: Kingdom Hall of Jehovah's Witnesses.

EXAMINER: How long have you been a member of this church?

SUSAN: Since 2009. I sent a letter from my church with my application.

EXAMINER: OK. I see it here. All right. You will say some things differently at the oath ceremony because of your religion.

◉ What Will You Say?

Do you believe in the Constitution and form of government of the U.S.?

Do you understand the Oath of Allegiance? Can you put it in your own words?
What does it mean?

Are you willing to take the full Oath of Allegiance to the U.S.?

Are you willing to bear arms on behalf of the U.S.?
If you were needed, would you fight in a war for the U.S.?

Are you willing to perform noncombatant services in the Armed Forces of the U.S.?
Would you work in the Armed Forces if you didn't have to carry a gun?

Are you willing to perform work of national importance under civilian direction?
Would you help your country in an emergency?

Your Form

Answer **Item Numbers 45. - 50.** If you answer "No" to any of these questions, include a typed or printed explanation on additional sheets of paper and provide any evidence to support your answers.

45.	Do you support the Constitution and form of Government of the United States?	☐ Yes ☐ No
46.	Do you understand the full Oath of Allegiance to the United States?	☐ Yes ☐ No
47.	Are you willing to take the full Oath of Allegiance to the United States?	☐ Yes ☐ No
48.	If the law requires it, are you willing to bear arms on behalf of the United States?	☐ Yes ☐ No
49.	If the law requires it, are you willing to perform noncombatant services in the U.S. armed forces?	☐ Yes ☐ No
50.	If the law requires it, are you willing to perform work of national importance under civilian direction?	☐ Yes ☐ No

N-400 Parts 13, 14, and 15
Signatures

 ## Listen to Hai

I understand English. I filled out my application by myself, and I didn't need a translator. I checked box A to show that no one else filled out my form for me. Then I signed my name to say that everything I wrote on the form is true. I didn't lie about anything. When I sign, I give USCIS permission to check the information and find out if it is true.

I have to sign my full name. I also write today's date.

Hai's Form

Part 13. Applicant's Statement, Certification, and Signature

NOTE: Read the **Penalties** section of the Form N-400 Instructions before completing this part.

Applicant's Statement

NOTE: Select the box for either **Item A.** or **B.** in **Item Number 1.** If applicable, select the box for **Item Number 2.**

1. Applicant's Statement Regarding the Interpreter

    A. ☒ I can read and understand English, and I have read and understand every question and instruction on this application and my answer to every question.

    B. ☐ The interpreter named in **Part 14.** read to me every question and instruction on this application and my answer to every question in ⬚ , a language in which I am fluent, and I understood everything.

Applicant's Certification

Copies of any documents I have submitted are exact photocopies of unaltered, original documents, and I understand that USCIS may require that I submit original documents to USCIS at a later date. Furthermore, I authorize the release of any information from any of my records that USCIS may need to determine my eligibility for the immigration benefit that I seek.

I further authorize release of information contained in this application, in supporting documents, and in my USCIS records to other entities and persons where necessary for the administration and enforcement of U.S. immigration laws.

I understand that USCIS will require me to appear for an appointment to take my biometrics (fingerprints, photograph, and/or signature) and, at that time, I will be required to sign an oath reaffirming that:

1) I reviewed and provided or authorized all of the information in my application;

2) I understood all of the information contained in, and submitted with, my application; and

3) All of this information was complete, true, and correct at the time of filing.

I certify, under penalty of perjury, that I provided or authorized all of the information in my application, I understand all of the information contained in, and submitted with, my application, and that all of this information is complete, true, and correct.

Applicant's Signature

3. Applicant's Signature   Date of Signature (mm/dd/yyyy)
    ➡ *Hai Pham*   08/25/2014

My husband helped me to fill out my application. He explained each question to me in my language. He filled out the application form for me. I checked box B, and I wrote the name of my language in the box. Then I wrote Jean Claud's name because he is the person who helped me fill out the form.

I signed Part 13. Then my husband filled out Parts 14 and 15.

I did not write anything in Parts 16, 17, and 18. I will sign them during my interview.

Susan's Form

Part 13. Applicant's Statement, Certification, and Signature

NOTE: Read the **Penalties** section of the Form N-400 Instructions before completing this part.

Applicant's Statement

NOTE: Select the box for either **Item A.** or **B.** in **Item Number 1.** If applicable, select the box for **Item Number 2.**

1. Applicant's Statement Regarding the Interpreter

    A. ☐ I can read and understand English, and I have read and understand every question and instruction on this application and my answer to every question.

    B. ☒ The interpreter named in **Part 14.** read to me every question and instruction on this application and my answer to every question in Haitian Creole , a language in which I am fluent, and I understood everything.

2. Applicant's Statement Regarding the Preparer

    ☒ At my request, the preparer named in **Part 15.,** Jean Claud Santos , prepared this application for me based only upon information I provided or authorized.

Part 13. Applicant's Statement, Certification, and Signature (continued)

A- 0 8 9 0 1 2 6 5 4

Applicant's Certification

Copies of any documents I have submitted are exact photocopies of unaltered, original documents, and I understand that USCIS may require that I submit original documents to USCIS at a later date. Furthermore, I authorize the release of any information from any of my records that USCIS may need to determine my eligibility for the immigration benefit that I seek.

I further authorize release of information contained in this application, in supporting documents, and in my USCIS records to other entities and persons where necessary for the administration and enforcement of U.S. immigration laws.

I understand that USCIS will require me to appear for an appointment to take my biometrics (fingerprints, photograph, and/or signature) and, at that time, I will be required to sign an oath reaffirming that:

1) I reviewed and provided or authorized all of the information in my application;

2) I understood all of the information contained in, and submitted with, my application; and

3) All of this information was complete, true, and correct at the time of filing.

I certify, under penalty of perjury, that I provided or authorized all of the information in my application, I understand all of the information contained in, and submitted with, my application, and that all of this information is complete, true, and correct.

Applicant's Signature

3. Applicant's Signature

Susan Santos

Date of Signature (mm/dd/yyyy)

09/16/2016

NOTE TO ALL APPLICANTS: If you do not completely fill out this application or fail to submit required documents listed in the Instructions, USCIS may deny your application.

Part 14. Interpreter's Contact Information, Certification, and Signature

Provide the following information about the interpreter.

Interpreter's Full Name

1. Interpreter's Family Name (Last Name)

Santos

Interpreter's Given Name (First Name)

Jean Claud

2. Interpreter's Business or Organization Name (if any)

Interpreter's Mailing Address

3. Street Number and Name

37 Lincoln St

Apt. Ste. Flr. Number

City or Town

Bridgeport

State

CT

ZIP Code + 4

01048 - 9634

Province

Postal Code

Country

USA

Part 14. Interpreter's Contact Information, Certification, and Signature (continued)

A- [0] [8] [9] [0] [1] [2] [6] [5] [4]

Interpreter's Contact Information

4. Interpreter's Daytime Telephone Number

2021120900

5. Interpreter's Mobile Telephone Number (if any)

3433433434

6. Interpreter's Email Address (if any)

jcsantos@dmail.com

Interpreter's Certification

I certify, under penalty of perjury, that:

I am fluent in English and Haitian Creole , which is the same language specified in **Part 13., Item B.** in **Item Number 1.**, and I have read to this applicant in the identified language every question and instruction on this application and his or her answer to every question. The applicant informed me that he or she understands every instruction, question and answer on the application, including the **Applicant's Certification** and has verified the accuracy of every answer.

Interpreter's Signature

7. Interpreter's Signature

➡ *Jean Claud Santos*

Date of Signature (mm/dd/yyyy)

09/16/2016

Part 15. Contact Information, Declaration, and Signature of the Person Preparing This Application, if Other Than the Applicant

Provide the following information about the preparer.

Preparer's Full Name

1. Preparer's Family Name (Last Name)

Santos

Preparer's Given Name (First Name)

Jean Claud

2. Preparer's Business or Organization Name (if any)

Preparer's Mailing Address

3. Street Number and Name

37 Lincoln St

Apt. ☐ Ste. ☐ Flr. ☐ Number

City or Town

Bridgeport

State

CT

ZIP Code + 4

01048 - 9634

Province

Postal Code

Country

USA

144 Parts 13, 14, and 15: Signatures

Part 15. Contact Information, Declaration, and Signature of the Person Preparing This Application, if Other Than the Applicant (continued)

A- 0 8 9 0 1 2 6 5 4

Preparer's Contact Information

4. Preparer's Daytime Telephone Number

2021120900

5. Preparer's Mobile Telephone Number (if any)

3433433434

6. Preparer's Email Address (if any)

jcsantos@dmail.com

Preparer's Statement

7. A. ☒ I am not an attorney or accredited representative but have prepared this application on behalf of the applicant and with the applicant's consent.

B. ☐ I am an attorney or accredited representative and my representation of the applicant in this case ☐ extends ☐ does not extend beyond the preparation of this application.

NOTE: If you are an attorney or accredited representative whose representation extends beyond preparation of this application, you may be obliged to submit a completed Form G-28, Notice of Entry of Appearance as Attorney or Accredited Representative, with this application.

Preparer's Certification

By my signature, I certify, under penalty of perjury, that I prepared this application at the request of the applicant. The applicant then reviewed this completed application and informed me that he or she understands all of the information contained in, and submitted with, his or her application, including the **Applicant's Certification**, and that all of this information is complete, true, and correct. I completed this application based only on information that the applicant provided to me or authorized me to obtain or use.

Preparer's Signature

8. Preparer's Signature

➡ *Jean Claud Santos*

Date of Signature (mm/dd/yyyy)

09/16/2016

NOTE: Do not complete Parts 16., 17., or 18. until the USCIS Officer instructs you to do so at the interview.

Your Form

Sign and date your form.

Part 13. Applicant's Statement, Certification, and Signature

NOTE: Read the **Penalties** section of the Form N-400 Instructions before completing this part.

Applicant's Statement

NOTE: Select the box for either **Item A.** or **B.** in **Item Number 1.** If applicable, select the box for **Item Number 2.**

1. Applicant's Statement Regarding the Interpreter

   A. ☐ I can read and understand English, and I have read and understand every question and instruction on this application and my answer to every question.

   B. ☐ The interpreter named in **Part 14.** read to me every question and instruction on this application and my answer to every question in [   ], a language in which I am fluent, and I understood everything.

2. Applicant's Statement Regarding the Preparer

   ☐ At my request, the preparer named in **Part 15.,** [   ], prepared this application for me based only upon information I provided or authorized.

Part 13. Applicant's Statement, Certification, and Signature (continued)

Applicant's Certification

Copies of any documents I have submitted are exact photocopies of unaltered, original documents, and I understand that USCIS may require that I submit original documents to USCIS at a later date. Furthermore, I authorize the release of any information from any of my records that USCIS may need to determine my eligibility for the immigration benefit that I seek.

I further authorize release of information contained in this application, in supporting documents, and in my USCIS records to other entities and persons where necessary for the administration and enforcement of U.S. immigration laws.

I understand that USCIS will require me to appear for an appointment to take my biometrics (fingerprints, photograph, and/or signature) and, at that time, I will be required to sign an oath reaffirming that:

   1) I reviewed and provided or authorized all of the information in my application;

   2) I understood all of the information contained in, and submitted with, my application; and

   3) All of this information was complete, true, and correct at the time of filing.

I certify, under penalty of perjury, that I provided or authorized all of the information in my application, I understand all of the information contained in, and submitted with, my application, and that all of this information is complete, true, and correct.

Applicant's Signature

3. Applicant's Signature [   ]   Date of Signature (mm/dd/yyyy) [   ]

   ➡ [   ]

NOTE TO ALL APPLICANTS: If you do not completely fill out this application or fail to submit required documents listed in the Instructions, USCIS may deny your application.

Interview Results and the Oath Ceremony

Listen to Chong

I got a letter from USCIS. It was an interview notice.

I did not have good luck at my interview. I had a bad headache. I was very nervous. I could not remember what to say.

The examiner told me that I needed to study more English. He said I could come for another interview later. I went home sad that day.

Three months later, I got another interview notice. I went to USCIS for a second interview. I had a different examiner this time. I was a little nervous, but I tried to answer the questions.

The examiner said that my English was OK. She told me that I would become a citizen soon. I was very happy!

◉ Listen to Maria

I spent a lot of time getting ready for my interview. When I got to the USCIS office, I knew what to expect.

I was nervous, but I answered the questions as well as I could. The examiner asked me to look at my application again to make sure everything was right. He asked me to sign the application again. I signed my photographs and another paper too.

He told me that my application had no problems and that I would become a citizen soon. I was so happy!

A few weeks later, I got a letter about my oath ceremony. I went to a courthouse to be sworn in. There were a lot of people. A judge talked about what it means to be a citizen.

Then we stood up and raised our right hands. The judge read the Oath of Allegiance. We repeated the words after him.

They gave each new citizen a Certificate of Naturalization. I will remember that day forever. It was a very important day in my life.

Next Steps

◉ What Will You Do Next?

I will register to vote.

I will bring my sisters to America.

I will get a U.S. passport.

I will study more English and get my GED.

I will get citizenship papers for my children.

Let's have a party to celebrate!

◉ What About You?

What will you do after you become a citizen?

Words to Remember

Study These Words

Here are some words that you might hear in an interview or read on the N-400 form. You don't need to know how to pronounce or spell these words. But it is good to understand these words. Read each word and the example that follows it.

It might help you to write the words in your own language. You might want to ask a friend to help you translate the words. Or you can use a bilingual dictionary.

accommodation

- I am asking the examiner to make an **accommodation.**
- I am asking the examiner to do my interview a little differently because I have a disability.

adopted

- My parents **adopted** me when I was 10 years old.
- I did not have a mother or father, so a new family took me in when I was 10 years old.

advocated

- Sulim **advocated** the overthrow of his country's government.
- Sulim told people they should get rid of their country's leaders.

against the law

- Selling drugs is **against the law.**
- The government says it is not OK to sell drugs.

alias

- Did you ever use an **alias**?
- Did you ever use a name that is different than the name you use now?

apartment number

- I live at 36 Main Street, **apartment number** 34-D.
- There are many doors at 36 Main Street—mine says 34-D.

apply

- I want to **apply** for citizenship.
- I want to fill out the forms to become a citizen.

Armed Forces

- Were you ever in the U.S. **Armed Forces?**
- Were you ever a soldier in the U.S. Army, Navy, Air Force, or Marines?

arrested

- Have you ever been **arrested** by the police?
- Have you ever been taken to jail and fingerprinted by the police?

bear arms

- I promise to **bear arms** for my country.
- I promise that I will fight for my country if there is a war.

biological

- She has one **biological** child and one adopted child.
- She gave birth to one child and she adopted another child.

born

- I was **born** June 4, 1965.
- My life started on June 4, 1965.

changes

- I have made two **changes** in your application.
- There are two places where I wrote some new information in your application.

child support

- He pays **child support** every month.
- He gives money to his ex-wife each month to pay his childrens' expenses.

children

- Do your **children** live with you?
- Do your sons and daughters live with you?

cited

- He was **cited** by the police for driving too fast.
- The police gave him a ticket for speeding.

claimed

- Have you ever **claimed** to be a citizen?
- Did you ever lie and tell someone that you are a citizen?

combat

- I worked for the army, but I did not do **combat.**
- I worked for the army, but I didn't have to fight in a war.

Communist/Communism

- Have you ever been a member of the **Communist** Party?
- Have you been in a group that follows Chairman Mao, Fidel Castro, or Karl Marx?

compulsory

- Joining the Communist Party was **compulsory** for my job in Russia.
- I had to be a member of the Communist Party to keep my job in Russia.

continuous/continuously

- Have you lived at that address **continuously** for the last five years?
- Have you lived at this address without any changes for the last five years?

country of birth

- What is your **country of birth?**
- In which country were you born?

country of nationality

- What is your **country of nationality?**
- Which country do you belong to? Which country are you a citizen of?

county

- My town is in Hampden **County.**
- My town is in a part of the state called Hampden County.

crime

- Stealing money is a **crime.**
- Stealing money is against the law.

current/currently

- What is your **current** address?
- What is your address right now?

current legal name

- What is your **current legal name?**
- What name do you use to sign important papers?

date of birth

- What is your **date of birth?**
- In which month, day, and year were you born?

date of marriage

- What was your **date of marriage?**
- In which month, day, and year did you get married?

daughter

- Where was your **daughter** born?
- Where was your girl born?

dead

- My husband is **dead.**
- My husband is not alive anymore.

deaf

- Otto is **deaf.**
- Otto cannot hear very well.

deceased

- My parents are **deceased.**
- My parents are not alive anymore.

dependents

- My children are my **dependents.**
- I pay my children's expenses because they are too young to support themselves.

deported

- Have you ever been **deported?**
- Did a judge ever tell you that you must leave the U.S.?

deserted

- Raul **deserted** from the Armed Forces.
- Raul was in the Armed Forces, but he left without an OK from his supervisor.

detained

- Have you ever been **detained** by the police?
- Did the police ever put you in jail?

detention center/detention facility

- Tina is in a **detention center** because she entered the U.S. without permission.
- Tina is locked up in a place and she cannot leave because she entered the U.S. without permission.

disability

- I have a hearing **disability.**
- I cannot hear as well as most other people.

disabled

- My mother is physically **disabled.**
- My mother is handicapped—she cannot walk.

disposition

- The **disposition** of my court case is "not guilty."
- The judge decided that I was not guilty, and that is how my court case ended.

divorced

- My wife and I are **divorced.**
- My wife and I were married before, but we are not married anymore.

driver's license

- Do you have a **driver's license?**
- Do you have a card that shows that you are allowed to drive a car?

drugs

- I do not use any illegal **drugs.**
- I do not put dangerous things in my body, like marijuana or cocaine.

employer

- Who is your **employer?**
- Who do you work for?

enter the U.S. illegally

- Have you ever helped someone to **enter the U.S. illegally?**
- Did you help someone come into the U.S. without an OK from USCIS?

entered into marriage

- My wife and I **entered into marriage** in 2003.
- My wife and I got married in 2003.

failed to support dependents

- Have you ever **failed to support** your **dependents?**
- Did you ever refuse to pay for food, clothing, or housing for your children?

family name

- What is your **family name?**
- What is your last name?

female

- Susan is **female.**
- Susan is a woman.

file income taxes

- I will **file** my **income taxes** in April.
- I will send in my tax forms in April.

fingerprint

- A **fingerprint** check will tell USCIS if you have ever been arrested.
- USCIS will know if you've been arrested before because they match the marks that your fingers make on a paper with arrest records.

force/forcing

- My boss **forced** me to work late.
- My boss told me that he would fire me if I did not work late.

foreign address

- My son has a **foreign address.**
- My son lives outside of the United States.

form of government

- America's **form of government** is democracy.
- America is a democracy. That is how we elect our leaders and makes our laws.

former/formerly

- My **former** husband was a U.S. citizen.
- My ex-husband was a U.S. citizen.

gambling

- Have you ever had a problem with illegal **gambling?**
- Have you ever played cards or other games, in a secret place, to win money?

gender

- Check the box to tell your **gender.**
- Check the "M" box or the "F" box to tell whether you are a man or a woman.

genocide

- The soldiers committed **genocide** by killing everyone in the village.
- The soldiers committed a terrible crime when they killed everyone in the village.

given name

- My **given name** is Lisa.
- My first name is Lisa.

guerilla group

- Eng belonged to a **guerilla group** in Cambodia.
- Eng belonged to a group that fought against the government in Cambodia.

habitual drunkard

- Albert is a **habitual drunkard.**
- Albert drinks a lot of alcohol every day.

hard of hearing

- Otto is **hard of hearing.**
- Otto does not hear very well.

height

- My **height** is 5 feet and 2 inches.
- I am 5 feet and 2 inches tall.

home address

- Tell me your **home address.**
- Tell me where you live.

human rights

- When Joseph forced children to be soldiers, he took away their **human rights.**
- When Joseph forced children to be soldiers, he took away the freedoms that all people are born with.

identification

- I use my driver's license for **identification.**
- I use my driver's license to show who I am.

illegal/illegally

- It is **illegal** to drive without a license.
- The government says that it is not OK for people to drive without a license.

immigration status

- What is your **immigration status?**
- Are you a permanent resident, a visitor, or a citizen?

income tax

- I pay **income taxes.**
- I give part of the money from my job to the government.

insurgent group/insurgent organization

- Joseph is the leader of an **insurgent organization.**
- Joseph is the leader of a group that is fighting against the government of his country.

interpreter

- Susan's husband was her **interpreter.**
- Susan's husband explained the form so Susan could understand it in her own language.

interview notice

- Do you have your **interview notice?**
- Do you have your USCIS appointment letter?

labor camp

- Sung-ho was the leader of a **labor camp.**
- Sung-ho ran a kind of prison where people were forced to work like slaves.

lawful permanent resident

- I am a **lawful permanent resident.**
- I have a green card. USCIS says it is OK for me to stay in the U.S.

lawyer

- If you have ever been arrested, you should talk to a **lawyer** before you apply for citizenship.
- If you have ever been arrested, you should talk to an expert who knows about the laws before you apply for citizenship.

leave

- When did you **leave** the U.S.?
- When did you go outside of the U.S.?

left

- Have you **left** the U.S. since you became a permanent resident?
- Have you gone outside of the U.S. since you got your green card?

legally incompetent

- Have you ever been declared **legally incompetent?**
- Did a judge ever decide that you needed another person to make decisions for you because of a mental problem?

lie/lied

- Jorge **lied** on his application.
- Jorge did not tell the truth on his application.

location

- In what **location** did you become a citizen?
- Where did you become a citizen?

maiden name

- Gina Garcia is my **maiden name.**
- Gina Garcia is the name I used before I was married.

mailing address

- Do you have a separate **mailing address?**
- Do you have a different address where you receive mail?

male

- Hai is **male.**
- Hai is a man.

marital status

- What is your **marital status?**
- Are you married, single, divorced, or widowed?

marriage

- Their **marriage** ended in 1998.
- They got divorced in 1998.

married

- Are you **married?**
- Do you have a husband or wife?

member

- Are you a **member** of any organizations?
- Do you belong to any organizations?

mental/mentally

- Karen is in a **mental** hospital.
- Karen is in a hospital for people who are having problems thinking or understanding what is happening to them.

middle name

- I do not have a **middle name.**
- There is no other name between my first name and my last name.

military unit

- Sergei was part of a **military unit.**
- Sergei was a soldier in the army.

militia

- Tomas was not in the army, but he belonged to a **militia.**
- Tomas belonged to a group that acted like an army, but it was not a real army.

missing

- My son is **missing.**
- I do not know where my son is living now.

N-400 application

- My husband helped me with my **N-400 application.**
- My husband helped me with my citizenship papers for USCIS.

nationality

- I am from Mexico.
- My **nationality** is Mexican.

Nazi

- Did you ever work with the **Nazi** Party of Germany?
- Did you ever work for Hitler's government in Germany?

nonresident

- Mohammed filed his taxes as a **nonresident.**
- When Mohammed filed his taxes, he said that he did not live in the U.S.

Oath of Allegiance

- When I became a citizen, I took an **Oath of Allegiance.**
- When I became a citizen, I promised, in front of a judge, to make the U.S. my number one country.

obtain immigration benefits

- Lara married a citizen so she could **obtain immigration benefits.**
- Lara married a citizen so she could get a green card.

obtain public benefits

- Luc lied so he could **obtain public benefits.**
- Luc lied on his application for food stamps and public housing.

occupation

- What is your **occupation?**
- What do you do at your job?

only

- Was this your **only** marriage?
- Have you had just one husband and no others?

organization

- I belong to an **organization** for students.
- I belong to a group of people who are students.

other

- Do you have any **other** jobs?
- Do you have any jobs besides the one you told me about?

overthrow a government

- Joseph's group wanted to **overthrow** the **government** of his country.
- Joseph's group wanted to get rid of the old government and put in new leaders.

owe

- I **owe** some tax money to the government.
- I have not paid the government all of my taxes.

paramilitary unit

- Tomas was a soldier in a **paramilitary unit.**
- Tomas was a soldier in a group that acted like the army, but it was not the real army.

passport

- I want to have a U.S. **passport.**
- I want to have U.S. travel papers.

permanent resident

- I am a **permanent resident.**
- I have a green card, and USCIS says that I can stay in the U.S.

permanent resident card

- I got my **permanent resident card** in 2012.
- I got my green card in 2012.

persecuted

- Have you ever **persecuted** another person because of religion?
- Have you ever hurt or made trouble for other people because you did not like their religion?

physical address

- I get my mail at the post office, but my **physical address** is 25 Main Street.
- I get my mail at the post office, but the place where I live is 25 Main Street.

position

- What is your **position** at United Paper Company?
- What job do you do at United Paper Company?

pounds

- Hai weighs 170 **pounds.**
- Hai weighs 68 kilograms.

practice religion

- Maria **practices** her **religion** every Sunday.
- Maria goes to church and prays every Sunday.

present/presently

- Are you **presently** employed?
- Are you employed right now?

previous/previously

- My **previous** address was 109 Harding Street.
- 109 Harding Street is the address I lived at before the one I am at now.

prior spouse

- My **prior spouse** lives in Mexico.
- My ex-wife lives in Mexico.

prison

- I have never been in **prison.**
- I have never been taken to jail by the police.

procured someone for prostitution

- John **procured** a woman **for prostitution.**
- John paid a woman to sleep with him.

promise

- Do you **promise** to tell the truth?
- Are you sure that you are going to tell the truth?

prostitute

- John hired a **prostitute.**
- John paid a woman to sleep with him.

provide

- Tomas **provided** guns to the people in his militia.
- Tomas gave guns to the people in his group of fighters.

rebel group

- Bernard was the leader of a **rebel group** in Rwanda.
- Bernard was the leader of an army that fought against the government of Rwanda.

register

- After you become a citizen, you can **register** to vote in your city.
- After you become a citizen, you can put your name on the list of voters in your city.

register to vote

- After I become a citizen, I will **register to vote.**
- After I become a citizen, I will put my name on the list of people who can vote.

repeat

- Could you **repeat** the question?
- Could you say the question again?

residence

- My **residence** in New York started in 2001.
- I started living in New York in 2001.

respect

- We must **respect** the rights of our neighbors.
- We must let our neighbors have the freedoms that all people want.

returned

- What was the date that you **returned** to the U.S.?
- What was the date that you came back to the U.S.?

Selective Service

- Every young man must register for **Selective Service.**
- Every young man must give the U.S. Government his name and address, in case America needs him to help fight a war.

self-employed

- I am **self-employed.**
- I have my own business.

sexual relations

- Husbands and wives have **sexual relations** with each other.
- Husbands and wives sleep together.

sign

- Please **sign** here.
- Please write your name here.

signature

- Is this your **signature?**
- Did you write your name here?

since

- I have been married **since** 1978.
- I got married in 1978, and I am still married now.

single

- Are you married or **single?**
- Are you married or not married?

Social Security number

- I have a **Social Security number.**
- I have a number on a card from the government. It shows that it is OK for me to have a job in the U.S.

son

- My **son** lives with me.
- My boy lives with me.

spouse

- Do you live with your **spouse?**
- Do you live with your husband or wife?

state

- My **state** is California.
- I live in the part of the United States that is California.

stepchild

- Linda is not my biological child—she's my **stepchild**.
- I am not Linda's father. Her father is my wife's ex-husband.

still

- Do you **still** live at 45 Meadow Street?
- Do you continue to live at 45 Meadow Street now?

support the Constitution

- I **support the Constitution** of the United States.
- I agree with the laws that tell how the U.S. government works.

swear

- Do you **swear** to tell the truth?
- Do you promise that you will tell the truth?

terrorist

- Carl belongs to a **terrorist** group.
- Carl belongs to a group that hurts people to get what it wants.

title

- Sir William has a **title** from the Queen of England.
- Sir William has a special name from the Queen of England.

torture/tortured

- Carlos **tortured** people to make them tell him their secrets.
- Carlos hurt people very badly to force them to tell him their secrets.

totalitarian

- Juan worked for a **totalitarian** group.
- Juan worked for a group that hurt people, jailed people, or killed people who did not agree with them.

training

- Sergei got military **training** when he was in the army.
- The army taught Sergei how to be a soldier.

traveled

- I **traveled** to Peru last year.
- I took a trip to Peru last year.

trips outside the U.S.

- Have you taken any **trips outside the U.S.?**
- Have you left this country and traveled to other places?

truth

- Do you promise to tell the **truth?**
- Do you promise that you will not lie?

union

- I belong to the Hotel Workers' **Union.**
- I belong to a special group for hotel workers.

vigilante group/vigilante unit

- Kevin's **vigilante unit** acted like the police.
- Kevin's group acted like the police, but they were not real police officers.

vote

- I will **vote** in the election for the president next year.
- I will make my choice about who I want for president next year.

war crimes

- When soldiers kill people in their homes, they are committing **war crimes.**
- When soldiers kill people in their homes, they are breaking the laws of every country.

weapons

- It is illegal to carry **weapons** on an airplane.
- You're not allowed to bring guns or knives on an airplane.

weight

- Hai's **weight** is 170 pounds.
- The scale shows that 170 pounds is how heavy Hai is.

widow/widower/widowed

- Are you **widowed?**
- Did your husband or wife die?

willing

- I am **willing** to follow the laws of my country.
- I agree to follow the laws of my country.

zip code

- My **zip code** is 22435.
- I write 22435 at the end of my address.